Praise for *DON'T FORGET TO SCREAM*

'Tells the truth of modern motherhood like nothing else I've read. Bold, brave and brilliant, it is also full of humour, joy and warmth. I loved it'
Cathy Rentzenbrink

'Honest, witty, powerful and moving . . . an important book brimming with hard-won wisdom'
Robert Webb

'*Don't Forget to Scream* is a stunning, urgent, feminist masterpiece. Many of the essays brought me to tears, and I had to give myself breaks between them to digest their beauty and wisdom and insight before moving onto the next . . . So many mothers will see themselves in this book. And anyone who has ever rolled their eyes while a mother struggles to get a buggy onto the bus needs to read it too. A masterclass in empathy. I'm buying copies for everyone I know'
Holly Bourne

'I loved these sharp, unusual essays about motherhood and cried my way through much of the book. Childbirth, desire, consumerism and marketing of baby stuff, deciding to have a second child, goldfish. Recommended'
Amy Liptrot

'Funny and heartbreaking – a powerful portrayal of all that makes up motherhood. It feels both intimate and profoundly universal'
Catherine Cho

'A work of painful genius. Exquisitely written, totally honest, insightful and alternately hilarious and moving. I don't have or want children and might not have picked the book up, thinking it's not "for" me. Which would have been a big mistake. Huge'
Jo Harkin

'Funny, honest, courageous and brilliant . . . I really recommend it'
Brian Bilston

'Extraordinary . . . I wanted to read it slowly because it made me feel so many things, but ended up devouring it because it's so damn good'
Emily Itami

'How I wish this book existed when I was a mother of young children. Each essay executes a brilliant swallow-dive from the enervating everyday of parenting into deep waters of profound and unorthodox thought. This is exciting, emboldening writing'   Tanya Shadrick

'An excellent book . . . elegant, funny, raw and beautiful. It made me angry with myself and the world but it also made laugh. Compulsive reading'   Emma Beddington

'Moving, funny, poignant and insightful: Marianne Levy's reflections shine a light on both the joys and lies about parenthood with which we're all complicit. This is *This is Going To Hurt* from the other side of the bed'   Dr Keir Shiels

'Deep, direct and moving but also wry and funny . . . intimate, powerful and painfully honest'   Beth Morrey

'Phenomenal. Words like "searing" and "extraordinary" and "blistering" will be used about this book, and they will not convey one tenth of the strength of it, nor the honesty or the bravery in writing it'   Emma Flint

'A remarkable book, cutting to the quick of what motherhood really feels like – the terror and the rage and the joy . . . shot through with calamitous love. I've read so much about motherhood, but I've never read anything as sharply honest as this'   Shelley Harris

'A brave, unflinching, utterly necessary book. I'm in awe of what it must have taken to write these searing and all too recognisable essays'   Tammy Cohen

'Perfectly articulates the contradictions of motherhood, the breath-stealing, heart-aching, painful intensity – and, above all, the love. What a book.'   Emylia Hall

DON'T FORGET TO SCREAM

UNSPOKEN TRUTHS ABOUT MOTHERHOOD

MARIANNE LEVY

PHOENIX

First published in Great Britain in 2022 by Phoenix Books,
an imprint of The Orion Publishing Group Ltd
Carmelite House, 50 Victoria Embankment
London EC4Y 0DZ

An Hachette UK Company

1 3 5 7 9 10 8 6 4 2

A CIP catalogue record for this book is
available from the British Library.

ISBN (Hardback) 978 1 4746 2365 0
ISBN (eBook) 978 1 4746 2368 1
ISBN (Audio) 978 1 4746 2369 8

Typeset by Input Data Services Ltd, Somerset

Printed and bound in Great Britain by Clays Ltd, Elcograf S.p.A.

www.orionbooks.co.uk

For R, W and O

Row, row, row your boat
Gently down the stream
If you see a crocodile
Don't forget to scream!

Contents

Introduction 1

Part 1   *If I Thought of Them at All*
          The Mothers 7
          Someone New 11
          Two Weeks 17
          Mr Skinny Legs 21
          A Quick Word of Advice 30
          Flesh and Blood 32

Part 2   *This 'Mum'*
          Brick by Brick 47
          Perfect 65
          The Garden of the Night 68
          Buttons for Eyes 80
          Bumbo 87

Part 3   *Be That Woman*
          Me Time 93
          High Wire 96
          Filth 103

CONTENTS

Health and Safety 110
Maths 123

Part 4 *The Book of Mummy*
Hand-Me-Downs 129
Some Discomfort 144
Press It 155
Bad Mother 158

Part 5 *Month by Month, Moment to Moment*
The Most Important Job 169
Zoom Zoom Zoom 183
The Land of Make-Believe 193
Summer 200
The Shape of Things to Come 206

Acknowledgements 223
Sources of Quotations 226

Introduction

My story is unremarkable. In 2014, I had a baby, my daughter. In 2018, I had my son. What followed was astonishing. At least, it was to me.

After the birth of my daughter, I tried to articulate something of what I was experiencing. I was met with well-worn assurances, with gentle concern, bafflement, indifference or disgust. And so I learned to stay quiet.

When a woman comes home from the postnatal ward, we talk to her about what we can see: the exhaustion, the mess and the paraphernalia. We talk about the baby, of course; this baby, just made. We forget that the mother is new, too.

I had not expected to find my voice the second time around. Even now I am unsure as to quite what prompted me to write a short essay and post it online when my son was fourteen days old.

People were asking me how I was. But instead of answering them honestly, I found myself protecting and reassuring the listener. I censored myself, questioned my experiences, even my thoughts. There were times when I feared for my sanity.

I was still weak from a difficult pregnancy, and ill with post-operative infections (although I did not know it) and I wonder now whether something of that attack on my system broke down a wall within me; I felt incapable of maintaining the calm maternal persona I had assumed when I gave birth to my daughter. Yet language failed me; I saw no way to explain what I was undergoing within the boundaries of acceptable conversation. Not to my friends nor to my family. Not to the health professionals whose job it was to look after me. Not even to my husband, the baby's father.

So what I could not say, I wrote. And the response to my words left me stunned. The strength of it! That so many felt as I did – the fear and love and the goddam rage.

That essay was 'Two Weeks', which has now found its way into this book. A short while later I wrote 'The Mothers', and in the weeks and months that followed, I wrote more and more. Back then, I had no intention of producing a book; I was simply trying to convey the meat and guts of what was happening to me.

I always believed that if I became a mother, I would be fine. That was when I thought about it, which I didn't, much. Coming of age in the 2000s, to me feminism was a given, as it was for most of the women I knew. If there had been difficulties for those who came before us, they appeared, from my standpoint at least, eminently surmountable. I had seen mothers, both real and imagined, all around me. Mothers in books, online and on TV, in newspapers and magazines; besides, I had a mother of my own.

Then I became a mother, and I felt as though I had been blown apart. And harder still, that I had to remake myself privately and hurriedly, while never allowing my smile to slip. I returned to everything I had read, asking myself, was I warned? Did I miss something? But no. Of the frantic horrors and unquellable panic, the sense that the woman looking back in the mirror was no longer someone I recognised, of love so powerful that it physically hurt, of the fact that I was utterly changed but in a way only I could see – I could find almost nothing.

Grief and falling in love, both are known to be universal, two of the great experiences of humanity. Motherhood is falling in love, and it is grieving, too. It is pain and beauty and death and life, all of it together. And I think, more and more, that on the page and in the park, in our homes and at work and in the corridors of power, motherhood's unvarnished realities deserve our attention.

Yet so high are society's expectations of mothers, and so uncompromising, that to speak of anything beyond milky bliss can feel akin to relinquishing one's motherhood altogether.

When – if – communication does take place, it is almost always from one mother to another. Even then, we retreat into familiar aphorisms and bleak jokes, into acceptable mummy tropes like the need for wine and the uselessness of men. We couch our words carefully, guardedly. 'I know I'm lucky, but . . .' and, 'I wouldn't change a thing, but . . .' or, 'Sorry, it's just that . . .' or, 'This is embarrassing, but . . .'

Looking back at what I have written, I am struck by how many times I, too, have apologised, for not saying what is expected of me. I am apologetic, too, for my white middle-classness, and this, I think, does deserve some scrutiny; I know that I have it good.

I have feared that my words will shock or offend. I have feared frightening people. I have feared being too loud, too angry, too much. In short, I have feared all the things women are taught to fear; things that, as a woman coming into adulthood at the turn of a new century, I had assumed we were, at last, beginning to vanquish. But there they were, just beyond my field of vision, low and scaly, waiting for me to dip a toe into the water.

There has been a global pandemic, and much of this book was written during lockdown, or in its shadow. I wrote never knowing when the next stint at my desk would come, during precious hours to myself, in the minutes between putting the pizza in the oven and getting it onto the dinner table. There were times when I thought that this book would sink me. Mostly, I think that putting words on the page is what has kept me afloat.

My children vary in age across these pieces, but as I finish writing, my daughter is seven and my son is three. So there are many children in this book – babies, toddlers and gangling kids. And there are many mothers, too, even if all of those mothers are me.

Part 1

If I Thought of Them at All

The Mothers

There's an email somewhere in the depths of my archive. I can't delete it. Nor can I ever look at it again. So it sits, not waiting, exactly. Perhaps it is bearing witness. At any rate it is filed away, invisible, but there.

The magnificent Anne Enright wrote that before she had children, there were women and there were mothers, separated by what seemed like a glass wall. When I first read those words, I thought, how apt. And then I came to realise that I hadn't seen the mothers, not really.

I had noticed them, of course. Mothers blocking the pavements with their buggies. Mothers filling cafés with their shrieking offspring. Mothers who had replaced their profile pictures with those of their kids, as though announcing their own obsolescence. Bovine mothers, rhythmically pushing–soothing–shushing, trudging laps of the playground. Gazing into the middle distance from park benches as their babies waved at the sun.

If I thought of them at all, it was with mild irritation. Taking up so much space on the bus and why can't they make their children shut up and who lets their kids run around like that anyway, and how come they get to dictate meal times and holiday arrangements and, oh, but how smug they are, how proudly complacent, how self-absorbed, the mothers.

We don't like to discuss how we came to be here. Have a car crash and you'll be going over it for years. Have a baby and no one ever need know anything beyond its weight and name.

When my son was born, I felt as though he and I had ventured to the frozen ledge where life drops off into darkness. A routine C-section under bright lights, the operating theatre was cold, a deep chill that ran into my open abdomen and left my little boy blue. It was a cold that worked its way into my bones and hasn't quite left.

My daughter's birth four years earlier was long and painful, and the inadequacy of those words in describing the experience still astounds me. It took fifty-six hours, and every second of each contraction was infinite. What's fifty-six multiplied by agony times eternity? If I had been able to walk, I would have thrown myself under a bus. When it was over, I had a healthy baby girl and I was a mother. Nothing had happened. Everything had happened.

And I was lucky.

Two friends were due to give birth on the same day. Their boys were to be like brothers. Only one lived.

A friend had a baby that seemed normal, until at eight weeks his development stalled. A few months later he was on the operating table, his brain filled with tumours.

A friend began telling me about her miscarriage with an apology.

A friend of a friend's baby lived and died on the same day.

A friend spent the second half of her pregnancy in hospital, where she bled and bled and bled.

A friend of a friend was pregnant with twins. One died, one lived, and she carried them together until it was time to give birth.

The friends who want children and cannot have them and are asked, *When will you have them, when will you have them, WHEN WILL YOU HAVE THEM?*

The friends who do not want children and are asked, *When will you have them and if not why not, why not, WHY NOT?*

I cannot think my friends are especially different from yours.

My daughter was the first in our NCT group to be born. We sent an email to our new friends with a few brief details – weight, name, Marianne's doing well (a lie, and one in which I'd already become complicit) – and a photo of our daughter, asleep. As the days and then weeks passed, other emails appeared, as one by one more babies came. A silence. And then, that final email. Tragic news. And attached, a photo of the baby, with some teddies, wearing a hat I'd given her mother a few days before. Her lips were blue–black. She was dead. She was beautiful.

I ran into the mother a few times over the next year or so. She became pregnant again and had another girl, and we pushed our buggies and chatted about this and that, trudging our laps of the park, invisible to everyone but ourselves. Eventually, I heard that she'd moved away.

I hope they are noisy with life and love and happiness.

I hope they fill the café, scream on the bus, block the pavement with joy. I picture her sometimes, in another park. With her new baby, a child now, and perhaps, some-how, her first girl, too. Running together across the grass, bright and vivid in the sun.

Someone New

Autumn is a season for pulling close. My children have collected all the cushions and blankets in the house, made themselves a den and cajoled me inside. It's hot in there, dark and cramped, there are far too many elbows and feet, most of which seem to be in my mouth, and of course, the kids adore it. 'It's like when we were inside your tummy!'

The process of growing another person has always fascinated me, that state between one and two. I'm hardly the first person to be preoccupied with the question of when life begins, nor have I ever felt possessed of any particular knowledge on the subject. But when reproduction moved from notion and into the foreseeable, I did expect some kind of insight. Here we go, I thought. I'm going to find out what it's really like to grow a person, to create life. In my mind's eye, I was standing at the top of a water slide. It was cold and it was high and there was elation and a fair measure of terror. Here. We. Go.

From the second we began trying, I was on the watch for the arrival of someone new, for the moment of my imaginings: the split, or emergence, the dividing of a cartoon amoeba. Maybe it would be at birth (although even then, I wondered idly, would it be when the head came out? The cord cut? When the baby was placed into my arms?) or perhaps it would be sooner, in the first definite kick?

One becoming two. Two! In my imagined future, the scenery might be different, and the props. My appearance would alter, but as an actor changes their costume, nothing more.

Like rainbows and boiling pots, epiphanies don't respond well to scrutiny. There was no moment of two-ness that I can pinpoint, no clean divide. And it's not a careful step onto the flume. It's more like being pushed, hard, from behind, and however long you've been standing there waiting, submergence in that icy water comes as a shock.

A few nights after I had taken the pregnancy test, my husband and I were shopping in town on a warm afternoon. *Dinner*, I said. *We have to go out for dinner. We've got to go tonight, now, I know it's only five o'clock*, I gripped his arm, *I'm not hungry either, but we have to. We must sit outside and it has to be perfect. Do you see?* I heard my voice reverberate across the square. *We have to do this now, because soon we won't be able to, because it will be winter and then there will be a baby and, no, I'm not crying, yes, I am crying, but what you need to see . . . is . . .* Here, I ran out of words, unable to articulate whatever it was. 'It' being hormones, blood, the rice-grain ball of cells that was her, singing a song I was yet to understand.

I downloaded an app that showed a picture of the foetus developing week by week, and for the first trimester, I came to see my baby as someone who lived in my phone.

Every morning I would wake, log in for a visit, and delight when a new week flipped by and it had grown from a worm into a peg doll, and then something that might, almost, be human.

Not long after, at the first scan, I saw our baby again on another screen, higher this time, facing out for all to see. 'Hi,' I said, and it seemed to wave back, although the gesture was general, and anyway, the baby wasn't really up there, but concealed, somehow, within my abdomen. It was there and it was on my phone, in my heart and in my head, someone about whom I knew everything and nothing, a sort of celebrity, or maybe someone I was stalking on Facebook. Poor baby, I thought. Could it not at least be left to grow those kidneys in private? The sonographer printed out a set of photos which I'd planned to put on the fridge, but instead kept in our bedroom to pore over late at night, the secret diary of us.

Hunger, exhaustion, a restlessness that sent me to do laps of the house at 3 a.m. – I felt them as my own even though I knew that they were not. Indeed, by the third trimester, distended and sloshing with amniotic fluid and extra blood and a whole entire child, what was left of my pre-pregnancy self seemed confined to a control tower, peering down from a high room atop the bustling factory floor. In photos taken at the time, there's a vast bump, but what I find strangest is my face, which is wide and somehow flattened. I looked like myself, and also not; a sister, maybe, or perhaps a close cousin. Despite being so expanded, I felt myself reduced to a flesh coating, pulsating, taut, a series of interconnecting tunnels, or maybe one of those modular hamster houses. Even my feet grew

bigger as my very ligaments loosened, as the boundaries
of my selfhood grew correspondingly slack.

They don't ping back, by the way. And I'm not just
talking about feet.

For the first year or so, according to the books, the baby
thinks it is part of its mother. My body agreed; not only
did the merest snuffle or cry send breastmilk dribbling
into my bra, but my emotions were hung upon those of
the shifting bundle in the cot. When there were tears,
I was frantic as a trapped bird, even as I tried to show
none of it; not to the baby, who needed smiles and calm
reassurance, and not to the people around me, for whom
the baby's crying was hard to hear but clearly not imbued
with the same panic-inducing quality that had me dancing on the end of its strings.

This ongoing two-ness was something I perpetuated
by wearing both my children in a sling, pausing occasionally to note that I no longer knew where I ended and they
began. Four of the last six years have been spent literally
unsure of how much space I have been occupying, first
swelling with pregnancy, then the sudden deflation, then
a baby strapped to my chest, my hands on a buggy or a
toddler on my hip. Crossing a room has required feverish
geometry, apologies, and scattered chairs.

Early on, my husband and I had a fight, the kind of
wild and howling row that is less an argument than it is
simply the outward expression of sleep deprivation and
fear. It seemed to me that the house was too much, too
heavy, too present, along with my husband, my daughter,
my own post-partum body.

I had to leave, to get out, now, but the baby could not be left, any more than I could pull off one of my own arms. I knew this without even having to think it, bundling my daughter up and out, stopping, when she yelled, to sit on the pavement and feed her, all the while inwardly raging, *I will never be alone again.* Then, a few minutes later, when my emotions had cooled, cautiously putting my hand down into the pram, *I'm sorry, I'm sorry.* Letting her wrap her tiny hand around my finger. I will never be alone again.

They are no longer babies, my children, and cannot remember their babyhood, though it feels so close, to me. Sometimes, that's what I long for, to feel the kick of my daughter in my womb even as those very same legs send her off across the fallen leaves and into the horizon, to feel the tug of her as she hurtles away. And sometimes, as small hands reach out to pull me back into the suffocation of their blanket den, all sudden yelps and sweet hot breath, I am assailed by a desperate desire for my singular self.

I contain my children as surely as I did in pregnancy. Contain them even though they are so clearly beyond containment; indeed, it is more like playing host to an occupying army. There are days when I stand amidst the wreckage of my former self and think that in asking, *How did I go from one to two?* I was posing the wrong question. The real mystery is this: how do I go back to being one?

For they are both with me always, my two North Stars. When I do escape the house for the evening, even as I relish the taste of the wine, the very adultness of the room, I find myself talking about them like someone newly in love, aware that for every mention of them that I allow myself, I must filter out three more. Later, on the Tube home, I thumb through their photos, woozily imagining myself climbing into their beds and curling around their sleeping forms.

It is rare that I allow myself to think back to when I walked the earth containing only myself. I want to stay here and I want to go back, just as, so often, I want my children to go and I want them to stay. There are moments, sometimes whole days, when I experience all these desires at the same time. So much want and all of it impossible.

It's OK, I tell myself, over and over. For even though I do not always believe it, I am allowed to mourn my old self. My one self. I should remember her; grieve for her. Shout goodbye to her, just as, every morning, I call out to my children from the gate. Knowing that they probably won't turn to see me. And knowing that sometimes, very occasionally, they will turn, and call back.

Two Weeks

There's a pram in the hall.

Well, really there are three prams in the hall. One actual pram and two buggies, which we've been meaning to put into storage and yet somehow haven't. Also, because we live in London, it's not a hall so much as a space by the front door.

This may not be especially coherent. Two weeks ago today, I had a baby.

Fourteen days old and he's tiny, still curled, his legs bandy from being inside me. Sometimes, when he kicks underneath his blanket, I can put my hand on my stomach and remember when only I felt him moving. Experience tells me that I'll forget it soon, that precise memory, maybe in the next few days. Right now, it's still there. Just.

The other night, I was crying, for some reason (you cry a lot when you have a baby) and my husband put his arms around me and held me close and patted my back, long and slow. We both realised in the same moment that he was burping me.

Mostly, we sit on the sofa, which means TV. Only, given my thrumming brain, there's very little I can stand to watch. Off the menu is anything with death, pain, tension, strong emotions, weak emotions, *any* emotions, animals, children and babies. Eventually, I discover a documentary on Netflix about pizza. When I watch it, I find its poignancy almost unbearable.

Four days ago (three? Five?) I went to the doctor, absolutely dragged myself in and sat down in the chair, more slumped, really, and said, 'I've just had a baby and I'm not well, I'm not well.'

The doctor was kind and asked what, exactly, was the problem. I told him and he said, 'Well, yes. You've just had a baby.' I nodded, because, of course, that explained everything. Also, I was surprised. I'd just had a baby!

I keep remembering him, which must mean I keep forgetting him.

Who forgets they've just had a baby?

We were in hospital four nights, and all I wanted was to come home. Then I came home and all I wanted was to be pretty much anywhere else. Days seven, eight and nine, I longed to run up mountains, get on a plane, go to a museum. Sitting in the same room, counting muslins and rotating bottles, I was frantic to fill my mind with something, anything. An exhibition, maybe. If I could just get up and walk to the Tube, I could go to an exhibition and learn something! In reality I could barely make it to the front door.

I was explaining this to a friend who'd come to visit, saying that every night as I lay down my mind kept flitting between the emptiness of the day that had just passed, and its ultimate triumph. All I've done is keep the baby alive / I've kept the baby alive. My friend told me the German word for precisely that Escher-like shift in perspective, and I was pleased, because on that particular day I'd kept the baby alive *and* I'd learned something.

I've forgotten it now.

People keep texting, asking, 'How are you? How was the birth?' I have answers lined up ready (like bottles – everything's like fucking bottles) but I can't tell them, not really. I don't allow myself to think about it much. The other afternoon, trying to nap, I remembered how blue he'd been when they put him on my chest, and how he'd stayed blue as the minutes passed, and the moment they'd taken him away, and the midwife who said, 'He's a fighter, he'll be fine.' I remembered thinking, *how the hell do you know he's a fighter? How do you know anything about him? He's five minutes old.* I remembered that, and how he had been inside me and then how he was far away, whole hospital floors away, and as I remembered, a drop of breastmilk, an opaque tear, ran down my stomach. I watched it in a detached kind of way, thinking that it was really a bit obvious that the milk should look so precisely like a tear drop. A bit much.

I know I've said it already but he is very small, unbearably small.

Because I had a C-section and so can't have a bath, and mainly because I'm tired, and busy not answering texts and lining up bottles, my body is still covered with patches of glue where they placed God knows what on me during the operation. Every now and then I find a new drift of grey gunge, on my shoulder or my inner thigh, and try to think whether I remember a sensor being stuck there. Two weeks in and I really ought to rub it all off.

I've been told to keep calm, even though our baby is so little and not gaining as much weight as he should, and outside it's a hundred million degrees and the newspapers say that when Brexit comes we may run out of food and the world could be ending and is, at the very least, on fire. A midwife comes over and asks how I am. I tell her that I'm suffering badly with anxiety. She nods and says, 'That can happen. Now, let's talk about cot death.'

When the panic comes, sometimes seeping in and sometimes with a smack, I look at him and think of the stillbirths and the miscarriages and the babies that will never be children and my breathing falters.

It'll all seem easier soon, they tell me. We'll be OK. He's only been here two weeks.

Mr Skinny Legs

A quick inventory of every Peppa Pig-themed entity in my family's possession:

1. One George Pig cuddly toy.
2. Two identical cuddly Peppa Pig toys. I have no recollection of how we came by the second, which leads me to believe that either I or my children stole it.
3. A Daddy Pig T-shirt, worn by my husband to children's parties, where it is much admired.
4. A cuddly Mr Dinosaur toy.
5. A too-small plastic cup featuring Peppa and George, generally used for dispensing medicine.
6. A Peppa Pig rucksack.
7. Peppa Pig-engendered arachnophobia.

What's annoying (it's all annoying) is that this last thing was not the outcome anyone intended; the TV episode in question sees Peppa and her toddler brother, George, encounter a spider, Mr Skinny Legs — so called, presumably, because even the word 'spider' is scary.

It's all determinedly upbeat. The little pigs search for Mr Skinny Legs, carry him into the garden and sing as he

climbs the water spout. So upbeat, in fact, that their attitude has caused problems in Australia, where Mr Skinny
Legs is not always quite so benign.

But before that, before all the singing and the jollity,
there is a crucial moment, the only bit my kids seem to
have taken on board. And that is when Mummy Pig sees
the spider, and, despite her best intentions, lets out a scream.

A few years ago, there was a bit of a hoo-ha after a midwife went on the record to say that it would be better if
women didn't quite so readily disclose, or seek out, tales
of difficult births. 'You just have to Google childbirth
and you're met with a tsunami of horror stories,' said
Dr Catriona Jones, a senior lecturer in maternal mental
health, by way of explanation. 'If you go on to any of the
Mumsnet forums, there are women telling their stories of
childbirth – "Oh, it was terrible", "it was a bloodbath",
"this and that happened". I think that can be quite frightening for women to engage with, and read about.'

At the time, I dismissed this as though swatting a fly; of
course we should talk! Of course we should be prepared!
It's only gradually that I've come to realise that I don't talk
about my first birth. Not to medical professionals. Not to
my parents and not to my friends.

Partly, it's a matter of time. The full story takes a min-
imum of forty-five minutes and very few people I know,
and certainly no doctors, have the inclination to listen
much beyond a quarter of an hour. Which is not to say
that they won't try, but it's tempting to speed things along,
or cut to the ending. Or (and this is understandable, but
not conducive to opening up) start getting a bit bored as

we plod into Marianne's Labour, Day Four, and pause the conversation to reply to an urgent WhatsApp.

Then there's the ick factor: blood and puke and shit, mucus and so forth. I was invited to a family party three weeks after giving birth. 'It'll be fine!' everyone said, and I didn't know how to say that I was bleeding, everywhere; that everything between my legs was stitched together, that my daughter was too small and I was too stunned; that something terrible had happened, something from which neither of us had recovered; that what we needed was to be calm, and safe, and quiet. Instead, I spent the afternoon nodding over pictures of other people's grandchildren, agreeing that I was lucky, that my daughter was beautiful, that it was all totally worth it, and wondering whether I was actually going mad.

And look: people just don't want to hear about a bad experience of birth. I have known people literally get up and walk away.

Before I discovered this, in those searing first few days, I did try. Just through the front door to visit my newborn, a friend, stopping by with a card, some biscuits and the most beautiful bunch of flowers, asked, 'How was it?' I started to talk, of the length of it, and the terror, and the pain; how understaffed the place was, lurching from crisis to crisis, and the netherworld that was the postnatal ward and – her hand went up to stop me. 'But come on. She's amazing, right? Just look at her. She's worth it.'

That phrase. I heard and read it so many times, and it always served its purpose, for the listener, at least. A kind of conversational dam, a plug to render me swiftly and efficiently silent.

At what point, I wondered to myself, would the experience *not* have been worth it? If I'd died? Well, even then, a life for a life, and a fresh, new, exciting one at that. Maybe if we'd both died? Maybe *that* would not have been worth it?

And, if neither mother nor baby exits this mortal coil, does this mean that horror can ratchet up to levels that would be unthinkable in everyday life, and it's still an exchange worth making; that it's all, basically, fine?

It does seem to me that this kind of thinking is what informs the delayed epidural, the women left to moan in corridors, the friend who gave birth in a hospital cleaning cupboard.

To say these things, to weigh them against the warm new life, a being that is not angry and exhausted and bitter . . . it's pretty much impossible, there, in the moment. It feels aggressive; it *is* aggressive, and aggression, rage, these emotions are, it has long been decided, incompatible with new motherhood. To rail against the fucking unfairness of it all would be to set up some kind of cosmic imbalance, a debt, somewhere, that must be repaid.

This is not an easy thing to point out to a kind friend, a loving relative, as the newborn snuffles quietly in your arms.

But even this, powerfully silencing as it is, even all this is not the whole of the story.

An intense fear of childbirth is called tokophobia, and, as you may have gathered, I'm a resident of Camp Tokophobe. Hell, I might be the mayor. It's on the rise, apparently, affecting 1 in 10 women. It seems strange, to me, that the number is so low.

After all, birth can hurt, it can really hurt. It can hurt more than almost anything, and if you don't believe me, then take it from Professor Irene Tracey, head of the University of Oxford's Department of Clinical Neurosciences, Nuffield Chair in Anaesthetic Science, or, in media speak, the Queen of Pain.

I recently read an interview in which she spoke about scoring pain on a scale of 1 to 10: 'I've been through childbirth three times, and my ten is a very different ten from before I had kids. I've got a whole new calibration on that scale.'

I guess I cite an Oxford professor because I'm looking for some kind of permission to say that it was really painful; and that's not good. Permission is something I find that I need, because to complain about the pain of childbirth feels petty. But it's OK to be scared of pain, isn't it?

And it's not only the pain. That whole 'pregnancy isn't a medical condition' line of thinking; the attitude of, 'it's natural, believe your body can do this.' It was never something that I could manage.

It's not that I didn't want to, it's not for want of trying, it's that such a school of thought was unavailable, to me. That chilling line in Adam Kay's bestseller, *This Is Going to Hurt*, about how human our doctors are, how they will inevitably make mistakes: 'One brilliant consultant tells her trainees that by the time they retire there'll be a bus full of dead kids and kids with cerebral palsy and that bus is going to have their name on the side.'

I couldn't un-know it, that 1 in 200 births in the UK

is a stillbirth. That, when it comes to the question 'Are maternity services safe?' between 2014 and 2016 half of all acute NHS maternity trusts were deemed as either 'inadequate' or 'requires improvement' by the Quality Care Commission (right now, as I write, it's 41 per cent).

Which of us, 200 years ago, would have died in child-birth? My two closest friends. Me, as it turns out. You?

I did try. I attended the classes, I breathed and I visual-ised and I tried to stay calm. It's just that one single piece of horror goes against reams and reams of trusting serenity. Slams into it, an iron fist into a heap of feathers. If some-one, however qualified, says 'it'll be fine' and I know that there is a reasonable chance that, no, actually, it won't, or that their version of 'fine' and mine differ by a margin that is, at the very least, considerable, then I am stuck, knowing too much. Just as, for my kids, Mummy Pig's scream negated everything spider-positive that followed.

How do you not feel scared? I go around and around, and I always come out at the same point, which is that tokophobia is a sensible reaction to a very frightening thing.

'Women with a high to severe fear of childbirth are more likely to have a planned or emergency caesarean birth, in-strumental birth and experience physical effects related to fear, such as a prolonged labour', says one study I'm look-ing at; say doctors and midwives; say NCT course leaders, says anyone and everyone, and for all my eyebrow-raising at the focus on breathing and the gentle music and essen-tial oils, I know they're right. I know, too, that I had no real faith that my body – healthy and functional though it had been until then – would know how to get a baby out.

I know that, and I also know this: that, in a very specific way, the horror that unfolded over those five miserable days between my first contraction and the arrival of my baby, was, at least to an extent, my fault.

Fear counteracts the hormone you need to give birth; it will stand between you and your body. Fear makes the whole experience worse. The greater the fear, the slower the labour, the more medical interventions, drugs, needles in the spine, tearing and cutting.

The more afraid you are, the more likely it is that the things you fear will come to pass. So, isn't it obvious? Just don't listen to the horror stories. It's like that movie, *The Ring*: if you put the evil DVD in the machine and press play, then frankly, when the monster comes, you were the one who invited it over.

Maybe I should have read less, known less, and trusted so much more. But on some deep level I find it unsettling that the aspects of myself I value most – curiosity, imagination, independence – are the things that may well have doomed my birth, have literally stiffened my cervix, rigid where it should have been soft, where *I* should have been soft, gentle, innocent; things that I am not.

Education versus biology; it's reminiscent of the wall so many women come up against, putting their desire to learn and to be autonomous ahead of starting a family, and, oh, now it's too late. I do not want to face up to the idea that what I have been taught to want – what I *do* want, mental freedom – might manifest itself as a physical barrier. Whether I face it or not, though, there it is.

So I don't speak about the birth. Because I think I

screwed up. Because I suspect that people will be filling in the gaps, thinking, 'Why didn't she try water?' Or, 'If she'd just done the yoga.' Or, 'She was never going to have a good birth, not with that mindset.' The sense of one's experience of birth somehow reflecting, or revealing, one's character, it's not true, it can't be true, and also, I fear that, at least in my case, it was.

Besides, what if I ruin it for someone else? On some level I do think, or rather, I feel, that my birth is infectious and that in speaking about it, my fear might spread, a creeping, inky bleed into the listener, jam her baby, ruin it all. It doesn't take much to plant the seed that will blossom into full-blown terror. Look, after all, at my children, screeching at even the remains of a spider's web.

And every time I hear how proud someone is of themselves, after having pushed a baby out with just gas and air, or how proud they are of their wife for enduring such a long labour so bravely, I think, well, I didn't manage, and I was not brave. I think that I deserve to feel ashamed, and I do.

A traumatic birth, and after, silence: what does it mean? This is what I ask myself, and the only conclusion I can reach is that it is something, and it is not everything. And I am talking about it now because if I don't, I fear something even worse: that I will carry it inside me forever.

Sometimes, I wonder whether there are more like me, with a large and crouching thing somewhere in their past, who've been taught to say nothing. Just the other day, at the school gate, I got chatting to a mum I don't usually speak to; someone we both knew had given birth, and I asked her about the experience of her own. 'Oh, it was awful,' she said. 'It's why I only have one. But, you know, it's fine.'

'Is it?' I said.

She thought for a moment. 'No.'

It might be that I regret this. Speaking now, seven years on, raking over the past, stirring up memories that should have been allowed to fade.

They haven't faded. They are as raw and as fresh as when I took my first careful steps from the hospital foyer into the waiting cab. I wish I had known then just how long it would take me to talk about what had happened; wish I had known how quickly and comprehensively I would learn silence.

And I wish I'd been like Mummy Pig. That before all the other stuff, the careful stuff, the correct stuff, I'd taken a moment to say how I really felt. That I'd been given the space and the permission, in those first few weeks and months, when I smiled, and was gentle, and soft, and loving, and grateful. I wish, more than anything, that I'd taken a moment to scream.

A Quick Word of Advice

He shouldn't be crying like that You're making a rod for your own back Be gentle with each other Babies cry it's what they do Have you tried co-sleeping You're going to be such a good mother If he's hungry he'll eat Pregnancy isn't a medical issue Fresh air will lift even the worst mood If your baby is healthy that's all that matters This too shall pass Get some sleep now, you'll need it Don't try to be perfect Try to enjoy it Follow your baby's lead Don't be afraid to ask for help Just try to relax Don't read too many parenting books Take lots of photos Skin-to-skin is so important You should breastfeed for at least the first six months You'll know when it's your baby crying Don't worry if the house is a tip Happy Mum happy baby The moment you hold your baby it'll all be worth it Cherish every second It's OK to cry sometimes Embrace it all That's such a boy bump You've got to have another Sleep when the baby sleeps You'll miss this Just wait until she's a teenager It never did us any harm Having a baby completes you It's a marathon not a sprint Learn to be flexible Try to keep a sense of humour Stay positive It could be worse at least you're not a refugee Giving birth is the most natural thing in the world Have you made some mum friends Pick your battles Don't co-sleep you'll never get them out again The days are long but the years are short You've got to go out just the two of you Someone needs a feed Trust your instincts It goes so fast No one has it all Don't nag he's doing his best She's a daddy's girl isn't she She'll sleep when she's ready It's just a phase You'll miss these cuddles Choose to see the good stuff We never did that in our day He wants to go back to Mummy Do what comes naturally You're his mother after all Make time for your partner Try not to look at your phone too much Do one thing every day Don't wish this time away I bet you've forgotten what it was like before you had her You've got to laugh haven't you Count your blessings Men are useless Trust yourself We potty-trained her at two It's not like it's forever It puts everything into perspective doesn't it Can't your parents help Let the magic in I thought this was what you wanted You can't have your cake and eat it you know Get your husband to babysit This has got to stop Every mother goes through this You'll have to learn some patience Don't take it personally Count to ten Celebrate the little achievements Surrender to the chaos You think it's tough now just you wait Remember your pelvic floor You never stop worrying Try to make the most of it Learn to accept help Children need to be listened to Enjoy the newborn stage Time flies Learn to have fun with them Remember you're the only mother she'll ever have A lot of people can't have children The day your baby is born is the best day of your life You must be so happy

Flesh and Blood

'I will eat you!' I tell my son. We're playing tickles on the sofa and his top is rumpled, revealing an expanse of squidgy tummy. I put my face right in there and blow raspberries in his belly button. 'I will eat you all up!' I say, and he screams with delight. 'Yum, yum, yum!'

Children and babies are delicious. They are sweet; the satin of their skin, their cheeks fresh and plump. God, they smell wonderful, better than flowers and food, and certainly better than sex; at once wholesome and intoxicating. Unwrap a baby in a warm room and it is like taking a draught of love potion.

Which maybe goes some way towards explaining why there is a lot of eating children in fairy stories. By 'a lot' I suppose I mean, one wouldn't expect there to be any, so every time it happens it's a bit of a shock. The oven being readied for Hansel and Gretel, the taste of gingerbread still on their lips. Little Red Riding Hood, peering down into the panting heat of the wolf's mouth. That my daughter remains sanguine in the face of these tales is a continuing mystery.

Perhaps young children are just accustomed to being

squished and nibbled and sniffed. Before I became pregnant, this was something I thought about a lot. The nuzzling and the stroking. The delight. I never knew quite what to do with these displays of affection, especially when they happened right in front of me. The extraordinary intimacy of it always made me uncomfortable. Am I allowed to talk? Should I . . . maybe . . . leave the room?

It's hard to throw off the filters put in place to ensure that when we do copulate and defecate, it is in a manner that sets us apart from the rest of nature – in private. Indeed, so private do we keep these activities that our lives are spent mostly unaware that we are animals. All of which makes the earliest weeks of motherhood a resounding clash of our public and private selves. Or, to put it another way, my nipples were somehow everywhere, intruding on conversations with friends and rendering tender photos unshareable.

'I'm afraid I can't stay in here,' a family friend told me as I lifted my top, making his way from the room as ostentatiously as he could. When the feed was over, and he'd been notified that it was safe to return, we regarded each other across my tiny daughter. That week there'd been a fuss about a woman who had been asked to breastfeed under a napkin in Claridge's, and he needed to make it clear whose side he was on.

'I suppose you support her,' he said. 'I suppose you think it's fine.'

'Where should she have gone?' I asked.

'The ladies!'

'I see,' I said. 'And do you generally eat your lunch in

33

a toilet?' I felt the room chill around me, could sense that such spite was unbecoming from a new mother.

But honestly, if I said I hadn't internalised this stuff, I'd be lying. Of course I have. Who hasn't? We teach our children, and ourselves, that every step away from our animal selves is an ascent of the ladder towards something higher and better. That there is more value in a sonnet than a hug. That adult tears merit sympathy, while a baby's screams are appalling, irritating, alarming, distasteful.

Even as I stepped across the threshold, I suspected that to enter into motherhood might feel like a regression, a betrayal of my mind, my autonomy – perhaps, dare I say it, my feminism, plunging myself deep into the patri-archy's maw. Despite my loathing of everyone who so much as dared to look away when I unhooked my bra, I do have sympathy (not much, and only up to a point) with those who find it uncomfortable. So much love, so much intimacy, and all of it just there, out on display, reminding everyone in the room that we are not creatures of pure intellect. We are messy. We leak. We are puke and shit and mucus and marrow.

I am not an animal, I wanted to tell people, as my daughter latched and I felt the twist-pain of milk letting down, the thirst that left me groping for a water bottle as my baby sucked and clung. I know it looks that way, but I'm *not*.

'Don't forget to make time for each other,' say the books. 'Take your partner to a restaurant. See a film. Go to a gallery, or out for a walk. Try to remember what it was that first drew you together.'

I chose the Wildlife Photographer of the Year exhibition partly because I am bad at looking at art. I imagine you are different, but when I stand in front of a Vermeer I don't know what I should be thinking. Something about the slant of the light, coming down from that high window? Its delicate caress upon cheek and neck? Well, all right, but I probably can't do this for more than a minute, two at most, before I'm distracted by literally anything else. It feels like a personal failure – that I can stand a metre from one of the world's greatest paintings and be locked in an internal debate over whether I will have a scone when I finally get to the café, or really go for it and get a Bakewell tart.

When it comes to wildlife, though, I'm easily enchanted. Living deep in the city means even a photograph of a dragonfly perching on a reed has the frisson of the exotic. And, unlike, say, Vermeer, this exhibition is clear in what it wants from the observer. Be awed by the texture of an elephant's ear! Laugh at the expression of a charismatic sea horse! And I do.

So this exhibition was a sure-fire pleasure, and I had been planning it with the gleeful precision of a four-year-old anticipating Christmas morning in March. My girl was old enough to go on a playdate, my youngest not so much a baby as a toddler, and while none of this had, thus far, translated into the freedom I had been promised by those whose babies had now definitely become kids, through calling in favours and some rigorous admin, I had scored us a single golden child-free afternoon. I would be astonished by nature and I would transcend my motherhood. And then I'd go and have that scone.

Which is why I was not prepared for the photo I encountered that day almost as soon as I went in. It took me
a moment to understand what I was seeing before I turned
away, perhaps even shielding my face. Now I know that
two minutes in front of a painting is plenty. When it
came to this particular image, I could barely manage two
seconds.

The caption alongside it read, 'Kuhirwa, a young
female mountain gorilla, would not give up on her dead
baby. Initially she cuddled and groomed the tiny corpse,
carrying it piggyback like the other mothers. Weeks later,
she started to eat what was left of it.'

The picture, that text, they were – are – unbearable.
Horrific. I looked for just a moment, and in it, I experienced a sort of high-speed collision of identities: the
intellectual standing in a museum, in reverent hush, and
my animal self, reeling from the immediacy of that image,
of the small, limp arm, stripped of its flesh, the expression
in the mother gorilla's eyes.

My head, my hands, were shaking as I walked on,
thinking that this, whatever it was, had nothing to do
with my motherhood.

So why was I still thinking about it, days, weeks and
months later?

Why am I still thinking about it now?

They give you a spinal block when you have a caesarean,
so you can't feel much. There's what's usually termed
'tugging' and 'pulling', which is sort of right. Some
people describe it as though the surgeons are doing the
washing-up in your abdomen. Really, though, words

can't convey the experience of having your internal organs moved around. At least, no words of mine.

They told me what they were doing; or, at least, a sanitised version of it. The only point at which they did not have to explain anything was when they cut the bond between me and my son. I swear, I felt him go. It was a sense of lightness in every part of me, the blood running through my vessels faster and more freely as the heavy, beloved load of him lifted, a balloon leaving my grasp, moving up and away.

Perhaps my system was not coping well with maintaining a baby; my pelvis was pulling apart and I had gestational diabetes badly enough to be injecting myself with increasing quantities of insulin. It might have been that, or it might simply have been that in the stillness of an operating theatre, my stilled self (the epidural for a C-section is strong) and a body that was not in labour, my perception was focused in a way that it had not been during the birth of my daughter.

A few moments later, as I held him to my chest, I became aware of voices, talk of grunting and blueness, and he was borne up and away to the ICU, whole floors above, where he would spend his first three days.

'We need a dummy,' they told us, in the first hours of his life, while I was still in recovery. 'He's distressed.'

Fuck, we said. A dummy. We never packed a dummy.

(*You should have thought of a dummy, you should have known this would happen, and now he's up there, 'distressed'; don't even think what that means, this baby that you made, that is your responsibility, that can't breathe, is up there on his own and you are down here, can't even sit up, let alone walk.*)

'Go!' I said to my husband.

'Where?'

'To the pharmacy. To the Co-op. I don't know. Go now.' Get out of this room, I was saying, I can't do anything, get away from me.

My husband ran to the pharmacy, ran even though the July temperature was in the thirties. Even so, by the time he was back, the baby had quietened, was no longer crying and clawing. 'He's calm now,' they said. 'Which is great.'

That it wasn't seemed apparent only to me. This wasn't how it was supposed to be – me, alone in my bed, while he squirmed away upstairs. Never mind skin-to-skin contact, between us there were bricks and floorboards and people, so many other people. A whole world full of them. How would he even know that he was mine? There had been a moment when he'd reached out, a vital window in which he and I were supposed to come to some kind of understanding of one another; that he would ask and I would provide. And in that moment, I was not there. Not me. Not even a dummy.

It was several hours after I had given birth, when I had been deemed recovered enough to be wheeled up to see him, that we were allowed into a room that was precisely warm and very, very quiet. Here, in the most inner of sanctums, nurses, doctors and machines performed a meticulous gavotte to keep the hospital's sickest babies alive.

The neonatal intensive care is known as the NICU, giving it the air of a grimly exclusive club, one to which my son had acquired full membership while I was still puzzling over the rules. Indeed, you have to get permission even to go inside, with the press of a buzzer and then a wait. The first couple of times I did it on my own, and when the disembodied voice said simply, 'Yes,' I didn't know what to say, managing only, 'I'm here to see my baby?'

The question mark enfolded within it not just my uncertainty about the entry system. My ownership of this baby seemed tenuous at best; I had no roadmap for the small and squirming life that had just been pulled from me. In my limited experience, things removed by doctors were always thrown away, with the exception of a tooth I once had removed from my palate when I was thirteen, which was returned to me, long and bloody, screwed tight in a plastic jar.

My baby, I remembered from the couple of minutes we had spent together, had dark hair. Looking along the row, I spotted a tuft of black brown, and I leant down and smiled and . . . and 'No,' said the nurse, stepping forward from the shadows. It was the wrong baby, of course it was. She didn't laugh.

I was shown to a box further along the row, as if I had reserved a puppy.

Here is your son.

When I look now at the pictures I took on my phone, to carry back to the ward in place of a child, I don't see him, at least not immediately. What jumps out are the tubes and machines, and the twin teddies on the plasters they used to secure the oxygen that flowed through plastic into each of his nostrils.

But none of this is caught in my memory. Instead, I was transfixed by the delicacy of his face. My baby was smaller than the first one I had approached. Just a few seconds later I was berating myself; how could I have thought *that* baby was mine? In truth, though, this baby didn't seem like mine, either. The child that had been inside me had danced with pleasure as I ate and woke me every morning with a thump to the liver. This baby, his movements as light as his delicate bones, seemed not so much flesh and blood as origami. His expression was thoughtful, as if this complicated business of staying alive was something that needed long consideration, even in repose.

What should have been my chest, arms and belly was, instead, the thin slide of a needle, a transparent polymer kept utterly clean and at ambient temperature. He had curled in on himself; whatever openness there had been had sealed over. A self-contained unit, in his plastic tank, within the careful quiet of the NICU and me on the outside, far away.

It wasn't just that my presence was unnecessary, irrelevant; the chaos of my maternal body was actually making things worse. Having not managed to produce a baby that could breathe for himself, not managed to pack the sodding dummy, not prepared for any of this, simply lifting him into my arms became freighted with significance.

When, a few hours after he was born, they handed him over, he was too small, the magnitude too great, the slash across my belly too recent and deep; I very nearly passed out. It was with frigid politeness that they ejected me from the NICU: 'Come back only when your blood pressure has stabilised, thank you.' Head lolling, I staggered into the corridor before collapsing into a wheelchair, a maudlin drunk on the street in Soho, murmuring to everyone and no one, *It's fine, I'm fine, I'm fine.*

After that, my battered body and unquiet mind seemed to accept that this place, with its stern nurses, the beeps and needles, mysterious fluids released drip by slow drip, was a better mother to him than me.

The days flickered past, stamped with words like 'tinzaparin' and 'colostrum'. I read once that after stillbirth, many mothers report that their arms ache, physically ache, without a child to hold. My baby was alive, and my arms did not ache. In honesty, I did not long to hold him; was frightened, now, by the mere suggestion.

They kept asking for his name. We knew it, had known it even before the birth of my daughter, so in every sense, he did have one. Yet I could not bring myself to say it out loud, not to him and not to the nurses. Not even when they glanced, meaningfully, at the whiteboard above his cot, which bore the words 'My name is' in Comic Sans, a font that seemed at odds with the atmosphere of the room.

'We could just . . . tell them,' suggested my husband. But giving our son a name, the bestowal of it, seemed too sure for the liminal atmosphere of the NICU ward, which was not quite death but not life, either.

'We'll name him when I can hold him properly, without all the tubes,' I said to my husband.

Then, a few hours later, a nurse asked again, and this time we cracked and told her. She seemed pleased, wrote it above his head, and went away. It was wrong, all of it, like a birthday present opened too early in a fever of excitement. We looked at the baby, and then at each other, and then went back to my ward.

And when they began to talk about returning him to us, it was clear, if only to me, that I could not look after him. It wasn't that I didn't want him, more that I did not know him, this quiet, frowning boy who was, apparently, mine.

I can follow the line of my daughter, her face, her personality, the very essence of her, and therefore, of us, right from birth until the present moment. It's harder, with my son. The galumphing, hilarious toddler he is today seems entirely separate from the tiny, serious presence in the NICU. In surrendering him to the plastic tank, I had lost the thread of him, somehow, dropped a stitch; as though he had been lifted from me too soon, his roots left hanging in the air.

Earth is a mother, and we, the mothers, are a kind of earth. It's there in the language, in words such as 'fertility' and 'seed' and – Lord help us – 'barren'. When my son was conceived, I called my husband at work. 'I feel a sort of stabbing, inside,' I told him. 'It's probably nothing. But if I get ill, can you remember that I said this to you?' I did not get ill, I got pregnant. The sensation I was experiencing was the embryo of my son burrowing into the lining of my womb. Implantation pain, it's called. The ball of cells, instructions for my boy, planting into the soil of me, ready to grow.

Our bodies are earth, and they are graveyards, too. There are the miscarriages we know about, and there are those that we don't. Think about it, all the women you know, and the pinpricks of light that shone, however momentarily, before fading out. The pregnancy test with the faint positive that is no longer there the following morning. The unusually heavy period, four days late. I think of what is left moving through us as molecules move through the soil, the slow release as cells part, letting go, spreading like ash, like stardust, before finally washing away.

They brought him to me and he slept. My husband left the room to get food and, eventually, I went to the cot, leaned in to see my son's face. His earlobes were slightly lifted, as though he was still crumpled from being inside me. I reached down to smooth them back, and they were velvet soft.

The room we were in was small, with one high window, and my memory has bathed us in the slanting light of a Vermeer, but I know it wasn't like that, not really. It was just a sweating woman with a wound across her belly, in a dirty nightgown, fondling her baby's ear.

That was years ago. Now, I pick my children over, smoothing hair, cutting nails, lifting testicles to wipe away poo; and I do so without thinking. I know them both, inside and out, every corner and crevice. The mother who kisses and nuzzles, who checks for accidents with a surreptitious sniff, she's me.

Look. I am a creature of words. I pride myself in it, perhaps foolishly. But here is something it took me too long to learn, and longer still to accept: love is flesh.

When I got back from our afternoon of wildlife photography, my kids hurtling at me as though I'd been away for a year rather than four hours, I wanted to tell them tales of crocodiles and neon frogs, for my mind to be filled with filaments and fronds. But it was the gorilla, of course it was the gorilla, whose image I carried with me, as she in turn had carried her limp child. Only now did it occur to me that the animal self might be a braver self. A better self.

For that tiny hand that could never hold back, she held it, and the cooling, disintegrating body, she did what mothers do. She carried him until she could no longer. And then she performed her final act of love. She took his flesh and placed it in the safest place she could, a proper burial, back within herself, to carry him with her always, in her guts and bones and blood.

I thought about her as I took off my coat and washed my hands, was still thinking about her ten minutes later as my son pulled me onto the sofa and lifted his T-shirt to reveal an expanse of warm tummy. 'Mummy. Mummy!'

I must have frowned, because his face fell.

'Yum, yum?'

'Yes,' I said, leaning down to press my face into his belly button, to savour every last molecule of him. To savour this, the high summer of our love. 'I will eat you all up. Yum, yum, yum.'

Part 2

This 'Mum'

Brick by Brick

The first day I was alone with the baby, I made a plan: we would go to the park. We would get there mid-morning, have a walk around, bump into all sorts of people we knew. Maybe someone would invite us for lunch? I strode through the gates as though entering the bar in *Cheers*. Of course, I knew no one, and was back home within the hour.

The day stretched on ahead, long and straight, as far as the eye could see.

'You could go to the park?' said my husband, when I phoned him in a panic, just after eleven.

'We've done that.'

A pause.

'I meant the other one,' he said.

I approached maternity leave as a sort of enchanted forest. Other people I knew had gone in and then come back out again, older and baggier; rueful; wise. One could peer between its trees, to see women in cafés, women in parks, occasional groups of women and their buggies clustered around our local bandstand, being shouted at while doing push-ups. Women whose engines had slowed to a putter, who would reach past me at the supermarket, or queue for coffee, always with one eye to whatever was happening beneath the pegged-on muslin sunshade. Mummies. Mommies. Mamas. Mums.

It was a kind of holiday, I'd thought, dashed with a little convalescence. The mother recovers from the birth, while the baby recovers from, um, being a baby. The mechanics of it all were never something I was much concerned with, in just the same way that I don't understand how derivatives work, or plumbing, or American politics.

It was sort of a job, too. After all, it came with money, regular money (for a freelancer, regular money is exciting stuff). It would shape my days for the coming year; my husband would go out in order to work while I would be on my maternity leave. 'On' implied something of a holiday, as did comfortable clothes and no boss. Plus, there was all that sitting in cafés.

The terms of this, I accepted without question. We both did. In a funny sort of way, it was nice. My usual job made people uneasy, for what, exactly, do writers do all day? Maternity leave: the words sounded good and solid, something we could all agree upon. And so when my first pregnancy was confirmed, with it were our plans for my year to come.

Here is what I think, now. Maternity leave is not a holiday, it is not a convalescence and it is not a job. It is no enchanted forest.

It *is* leaving; it is leaving one's old life behind.

★

What are you doing when you are on maternity leave? Everything, and nothing, and everything.

It is all the contradictions of motherhood at once. It is never being alone and being lonely as hell. It is unbearably tense and it is very, very dull. It is crying with love for the tiny person in your lap and simultaneously wanting to hand the baby over and run away to Paris, or Sydney, or Mars.

The thump–click as the radiators came on every morning, the different creak-note of each step of the stairs. Sunlight moving across the floor. My daughter's gaze, the black, Paddington-hard stare of a newborn, gradually diluting into a softer, and I hoped, more forgiving blue. Sometimes our eyes would meet, a junction of two interior lives. 'Come here,' I would say, even though she was already in my arms.

Breastfeeding, hour upon hour, as the television spooled through shows I'd been told I might enjoy. *Gossip Girl*, *The O.C.* and *The Real Housewives of Beverly Hills* chuntered away, someone recounting a complex anecdote from which I'd missed some vital early detail. My bum carved a dip into the sofa as I observed the wrinkles in the curtains, a spot where the decorator had missed his second coat of paint on the wall.

As a child, I had played dollies, and something of this returned to me in those first days alone at home. I moved with great care, cutting nails and changing miniature clothes with a respect of the sort I imagine a Victorian gentleman might have employed when rearranging his fossils or dusting a stuffed bird.

Until.

A few weeks in, while I was changing her nappy, a small hand was extended.

'Do you want to hold it?' I asked and, yes, it seemed she did. My baby wanted things. No stuffed bird, this. She had personality.

'Da,' my daughter said to me, one morning, smiling. 'Da.' Her voice was soft, flute-like, unmistakably hers. 'Da.'

'Da?' I said to her. 'Da?'

'Da.'

'Da. Da?'

'. . . da.'

'Da da? Da? Da?'

Oh, she'd gone to sleep.

'Da' was followed by 'ba' and 'ma', and now my monologues became conversations, of a sort. My daughter would chuckle to me, to herself; she would coo and sing. We played, upstairs in her bedroom, or downstairs, or on our bed.

'Now,' I would say, 'shall we go in here? Can you see the sky? Look at the clouds. They're moving, can you see? That's because it's windy. Shall we open the window? Can you feel the wind?' And she would blink and maybe say, 'Oh,' and I would wonder at the sound, so dense with meaning, so small.

All the while, she was cloaking the rawness of her newborn state with fat and experience. I shifted between fearing that her true self was being lost beneath clothes and toys and hair, and knowing that, really, we were uncovering her; that she was growing, filling out, becoming herself and a part of the world. The first time her feet met grass. The first time she wore trousers.

Look at you, looking at me! Rolling! Sitting up all on your own. Over we go. *Wheeee!*

As she grew older and began to move, we explored beneath her cot, between the chair legs. One morning, she triumphantly ascended the stairs.

This, I discovered, was a baby whose desires were not always the simple needs I had been expecting: sleep, milk, snuggles. No, my daughter wanted to spend hours examining the pebbledash of a certain wall, would scream if I tried to pull her away. This mushed-up sweet potato, yes, but absolutely not that pear. No sleep today, thank you. Sometimes, she would simply explode – *That's it! I've had enough!* – someone at the end of her tether, before yelling tears, on and on and on, inconsolable. She's not crying now, seven years later, so presumably it must have stopped eventually, but I have no memory of when or how this was achieved.

She, meanwhile, had a very specific mother, who was not quite like other mothers, or, at any rate, was not the mother she had been born to expect. Sometimes her mother was there when needed, held her safe for the hours she required. There was enough milk, mostly, although on some days it took much too long to come, tiny trickles when what she required was a full belly NOW! The face that smiled down at her, however – the mother face, the mother arms, they were stiff, sometimes, when they should have been soft, always.

And I regarded her narrowly, too, this new wife, this 'mum'. The household, with its husband and sweet baby girl, didn't seem to suit her, she didn't fit. Everything seemed fine – the baby, healthy and growing, the dad doting upon them both — but no. She wasn't happy, not really, not at all.

The moment my husband went back to work and I stayed at home, we were divided. I might say that we were a city, and a wall was built between us. In the earliest days, we could remember the terrain the wall crossed, the streets and the squares. We could shout messages to one another, could even run up to it, press our faces to the bricks, reach out in the hope that our fingers might touch.

'How was your day?' my husband would ask.

And I would say, 'It was hard.'

'What happened?'

'I put her down to go to sleep and she didn't but then she did.' Or, 'I tried giving her apple puree. She might like it, I'm not sure. Oh, and then she was sick.'

Navigating any one of these might have taken the entirety of my intellect, could have lasted hours; they were events of immense importance, and yet spoken out loud they appeared entirely trivial. When, a minute later, my husband would change the subject, I wanted to grab him by the shoulders and roar.

Then there were the problems beyond articulating, problems that sounded small but loomed confoundingly large: 'I wanted a cup of tea and I couldn't have one.' 'My boobs feel weird today.' 'That woman was in the shop again, the one who says nice things but doesn't mean it.'

Instead, ravenous for news of the outside world, I would listen to my husband's tales from work, the boss that said this, the deadline that moved, the endlessly malfunctioning printer. I would care, like I had always cared, and I would be sorry, or triumphant. I would care right up until he would try to set my day alongside his and I would think, no. Your troubles are not my troubles. I cannot even begin to hear, let alone sympathise, with your slight paunch, when my nipples are bleeding and cracked. Your printer problems are not the same as my inability to leave the house without forty-five minutes' preparation. Our days do not carry the same weight.

From trying to care, I moved swiftly into not caring whatsoever. Fuck you and your day in the office, I would think, wild with sleep deprivation and hormones and Lord knows what else. Fuck the canteen, fuck your colleagues, your work, your boss. Fuck everyone. Nothing is as hard as this.

And you know what, I would say, in my mind, as he took the baby from me, aiming the silent words hard and fast at his defenceless back, even if it *is* hard, at least you get to walk away. My work doesn't stop, not for one second, not even when I am asleep. And have you noticed that I don't sleep? Well, have you?

Yes, I would spit, silently, at the wonderful man with whom I had chosen to share a life, a child; yes, over the course of ten hours, maybe you had a couple of tough ones, but at least you could stand up, prepare food and eat it; go and take a shit when you needed to. At least you get to look down at your computer and see what you've done, see what you've achieved at the end of the day. At least. Your. Day. Ends.

I didn't say that, either.

What did my husband think of all this? I can't ask,

because I don't want to know. I can picture his face, though, the particular crinkle of his brow, as, after ten minutes of crying and a small but vicious fight, the creature that had replaced his wife said, brightly, with maybe just a shade of mania, 'Look! I bought a new kind of hook for the buggy!' before crashing off to bed.

The quiet, as I listened, for his feet on the stairs, for the squeak from the baby that would, within moments, become a raw and desperate yell.

Into that silence, I would mouth, 'Please,' or, 'Help me.' Over and over, I would try to put into words the dawning realisation that I could not do this, not even for another second, let alone six months.

But before I even came close to opening my mouth, I closed it again. The mortgage needed to be paid, my daughter's nursery place was booked for the week after her first birthday. I was her mother, damn it, and we'd agreed, hadn't we? If this was a cage, I'd locked myself in and handed away the keys.

And, of course, it wasn't a cage. It was our house, and in it, my kind, attentive husband, and my beautiful baby daughter, who rolled and sang and loved to burst bubbles and feel the moss between her soft little toes. I had work lined up ready, my friends were close by, and my parents were alive and healthy. In just a few months my maternity leave would end, and *they're only this tiny once, the moments are so precious and then they're over, gone, forever.* It would be wrong to wish all this away. Wouldn't it?

If there was a wall between us, I built it myself, brick by brick.

★

'Isn't there a drop-in group you can go to?' said my husband, when I rang him at work for the third time that day. 'A bump and baby thing, there must be one starting about now?'

'I don't know.'

'Then why don't you walk to Tesco? Go the pretty way. Maybe she'll sleep, and you can listen to a podcast.'

A trip to the supermarket via the park; what more perfect excursion could there be for a mother and her baby on a late summer's afternoon?

Even this, especially this, was to feel control sliding from my fingertips. For the next hour, I would be subject to the whims of the weather, to the temperature, the strength of the sun on vulnerable skin, and to the mood of the small overlord in the pram.

And if everything is aligned, and nothing terrible is happening in the precise and immediate moment, on to the next level of threat: that of each and every passing stranger.

Would they stop and admonish me for the lack of baby's hat, socks or sunshade? Would they be accompanied by a large and barking dog? Would they be one of those people whose fingers seem to slither into any spare patch of exposed flesh, never mind that the baby is sleeping . . . *What a darling, what a love. Got a good pair of lungs, hasn't she? She needs a feed, poor mite.*

They don't mean anything, I would say to myself, slaloming us both away. It's not personal.

Honestly, though? Yeah, they meant something. When they said to me, 'Your baby needs a feed,' there was kindness, yes. And there was a frisson of pleasure, too. Over and over, I caught the sting of it, the glee, the delicious spite.

Everywhere I went, it was there, the sense that motherhood elevates women, while simultaneously bringing them back to where they belong. Those of us with the gall to go out there, beyond the confines of our own front door, don't we need reminding of who we really are? Don't we need bringing down a peg or two? Education, savings, contraception, autonomy? It's all very well, dear, but your baby is what matters now.

This is what I felt. Whether any of it was real, or a projection of my exhaustion, my ambivalence and shock, I did not – do not – know.

But, look! Baby Massage, Songs and Stories, Baby Sensory, Sign and Learn, Soft Play. Places that had hitherto been closed and mysterious to me now threw open their doors. Indeed, they were the only spaces I was welcome, for when I attempted to do pretty much anything I had done before (go into a newsagent, get on a bus), it was clear, quite painfully and viciously clear, that these were not for me. For while babies and mothers are precious and vital and beautiful, they are also weird, too fleshly, too annoying. They are wide and ungainly. They tend to make noise.

In the months after I had my daughter, none of my clothes would fit. My maternity wardrobe had been bought for the summer, and when I held up the clothes of my old life they struck me as insane – an array of jumpers that could only be washed by hand, white T-shirts, a tiny pair of jeans. It was like I'd inherited the wardrobe of Miley Cyrus.

So I went to a shop, with the baby, and everyone exclaimed when we came in, and cooed as I thumbed the racks. And gazed at me in mute horror as my daughter went off like a fire alarm whenever I turned my back on her, raised eyebrows as I tried to fit her buggy into a changing cubicle along with the nappy bag and an armful of clothes and, oh yes, my post-partum self. 'I'll come back,' I said, to the lady behind the till, after my visit ended before I'd even tried anything on. 'Good idea,' she said, not even attempting to hide her relief.

The next day, I took my daughter to a bump and baby group, six minutes' walk around the corner. Packing, preparing and parking the buggy meant that we arrived half an hour late.

'*Oooooh!*' everyone cried, as I eventually came through the door, sending toys and changing bags and probably several babies flying. 'Your little one is so small!'

Yes, she was. Everyone else's babies were massive: two, three, even four months old, with thick arms and enormous heads; babies that could roll and smile and sit up unaided, the show-offs.

And their mums! If the babies were accomplished, then their mothers had surely been mothers always. I saw nappy changes executed mid-conversation with a single hand. When feeding time came, no in-and-out, in-and-out: nipples were parked squarely into hungry mouths. The way they rocked their grumpy babies, almost absent-mindedly; the ease with which they manoeuvred their tits in and out of their tops, unhooking feeding bras as though they'd worn them since puberty.

Afterwards, they peeled off in threes and fours to go for

coffee, and I watched and hoped I'd be asked along too, much in the manner I had back when I was fourteen and first saw a spliff being handed around at a party. Two of them were talking about the difficulty of using a buggy on the streets of New York, and it was like that bit in *Pulp Fiction* where John Travolta dances with Uma Thurman – utterly, unattainably, insanely, unbearably *cool*.

Live in a divided city for long enough and coming up again and again against the wall will hurt too much. Your feet steer you away from the dead ends. If you remember the things that lie over there – the restaurant with candles and white linen, say, or the quiet of a library – you believe that these are no longer places for you. You would not be welcome; you might not even know what to do. So you learn to live with who and what is on your side.

Before, friends had been for fun. During maternity leave, with my parents and my husband's parents unable to offer more than occasional companionship, and my husband at work from nine until seven, friends became as vital as air.

I made new friends, mum friends, and found that the conversational rules were different now. I had not, until this point, realised quite how much talking about work defines us. There was a certain sense of women whose edges had blurred, both in personality and in flesh. (With a couple of notable exceptions, we were all quick to point out that we were softer, squashier, than we had been; our clothes floppier, our belongings slung about us, dangling from buggy handles and occasionally trailing along the floor.) I only had the vaguest sense of what these women 'did' – and anyway, they weren't doing it and wouldn't be for a while.

There was no alcohol, not in that first year: deprived of sleep, we were drunk already. No booze for us breast-feeders, and no food that was rich or spicy, for fear that it might unsettle tiny tummies. Instead, there were biscuits and there was cake, both served with a generous helping of guilt as we surveyed our new bodies and spoke of our revulsion at ourselves, while simultaneously urging each other to take another slice.

Oh, the cake. The endless, endless cake. We made cakes and we brought cakes to each other's houses. We exclaimed over cake. Cake and cake and cake.

Sometimes, I thought my old friendships could do with a bit more of all this. There was a certain freedom, cross-legged on someone's rug, surrounded by biscuits, babies and cushions. We spoke of our little ones, of course, and then of our stitches and lacerated nipples, the state of our perineums and pelvic floors; after the first few meetings we were on to sex, in more detail than my eleven-year-old self, poring over *Cosmopolitan*, could ever have imagined.

All the time, I was regarding these new friends, taking in their opinions on weaning and the difficulty of shag-ging with a five-month-old next door, which brand of mattress protector is the best, and, 'Are you thinking of getting a Jumperoo?' I listened and tried, from all this, to extrapolate down and in, to penetrate what lay beneath.

Can I speak the truth to you? I wondered. *Are you here with me? Will you understand?*

There are things it is hard to say to people who do not have children. What is perhaps not obvious is that it is also hard – differently, but equally – to say these things to parents, too. To say, 'I have been diminished,' or, 'This is more awful than not,' or, 'I have exchanged myself for a baby and I resent it; do you?' puts the listener in something of an awkward position. These were women who had made the leap alongside me, after all.

Besides, I knew full well that not every new mother felt as I did. There are those for whom, in having a baby, the world finally makes sense.

To tell these women apart, that was the trick. To search their faces, run their words through a scanner, catch the phrases that might indicate they, too, were members of the resistance.

'I find it difficult,' I once managed to say. I had woken that morning with a new resolve. This would be the day I'd communicate something of what was going on in my fetid head. And this particular friend, I thought, might just, maybe, be on my side.

My courage had waned as the morning progressed, so the words had gone unspoken all through the decaf cappuccino and chocolate chip brownie, and now we were standing at the bus stop, and if I didn't say it, then I knew I never would. 'Staying at home with a baby, it's . . . so . . . hard.'

'Oh,' she said, perplexed. 'I love it.'

And that was that.

Sometimes, an old, pre-child friend would swing by, coming from Something Important and on their way to Something Exciting. The baby and I always tried to appear perky, which was doable, for an hour, and everyone concerned would politely look away from the skin that crept out of the waistband of the clothes I couldn't fit into, the occasional flash of boob or slosh of warm puke.

Look, I would say to my mother self, *hold it together, back straight, chin up.* Here is someone who remembers me from before you, someone who has come from the wide world, where bottles and sleep patterns and suchlike are not the whole conversation, are not the conversation at all.

Entire weeks would be constructed around such visits. I hungered for them, was well aware that my supply of friends was finite, intermittent, and could be turned off without warning. Once, after an endless spell of loneliness, the friend who had planned to see my daughter and me cancelled at the last moment, because we had been double-booked with the hairdresser. 'No worries!' I texted back. Just another ten hours without adult company, and no one even to tell.

When they did drop by, these friends from my other life, I didn't want to complain. Tears, sadness, rage – it is not much fun to be around, and I wanted them to come back, after all.

Most of my friends were without children, and I did not know how to articulate what was happening to me; was desperately afraid that if I tried, they would not understand. And besides, some friends, I knew, longed for children of their own and did not have them; it seemed wrong to appear even momentarily resentful.

How to say, to someone who has confessed how much they want kids, that you fear everything you were, that you are, has been bulldozed by the task of looking after your swiftly conceived, healthy, beautiful baby? On four and a half hours of sleep I had no sense of how to even begin to communicate the realities of my life without sounding ungrateful to the point of revulsion, a Veruca Salt stamping her spoilt little feet.

From the moment your bump becomes visible, you can hurt others without saying anything. All through my maternity leave I knew this, from articles I had read, message boards I'd strayed across, reading and reading, a kind of voyeur, looking in on the agony of others. I read Miranda Ward, who writes so vividly about infertility and her loathing of the 'mumsy mum' whose every gesture seems designed to cause pain. As exactly such a mum, I strove to hide how much I longed to sit in clean clothes and read undisturbed; to be a self-contained, singular unit once more. To be visible. To be more than just an annoyance, an obstacle, a piece of street furniture, a buggy-pushing drone.

Don't mistake me for one of them, I might have said, to Ward, to anyone. I'm not a mumsy mum. I'm not even a proper mother. I don't know what I am. I wanted a baby, I still do, and I want to be *her* mother, but not *a* mother.

These are not things one can easily say out loud. Not when your friend has an hour, two at most. And not when you have your baby there on your knee and a health visitor a metre away, doggedly berating some other unfortunate woman for introducing solids two weeks earlier than the guidelines stated by the NHS.

So instead, when people asked me, 'How are you?' I would answer with the baby's news, of which there was usually plenty. The baby's narrative became my narrative. Indeed, it was my narrative. Not the whole of it, but enough. Enough for everyone else, even if not for me.

*

Through all this, my daughter grew.

We went to the library, did circuits of the park, became regulars at baby cinema. One week, we saw the same film three times.

My phone was loaded with podcasts; my most intimate hours were spent in the company of US radio presenters who never even knew I existed.

I listened as we walked, and walked, through the neighbouring streets, as I developed a personal acquaintance with each individual flower. Day by day I watched as puddles rose and fell. Graffiti layered upon the railway arches. The ducklings on the pond fledged and flew away. The water, the sky, nothing passed me by; I saw it all.

Her face, most of all. We spent a year watching one another, my daughter and I, learning each other, forming a language all of our own. Once, when she was small, and crying, I took her from my husband and pressed her to me, just so; I knew she would quieten, and she did.

'How did you do that?' asked my husband.

I told him that I didn't know, that it was just a coincidence, nothing personal. 'It's not like I have some special power,' I said.

The power I had was not special. But it was particular, and it was very hard won. Even as I resented it, I gloried in it; even as I gloried in it, I was impatient with myself for believing it was an indicator that, as far as our daughter was concerned, I was, somehow, best.

She and I have a particular bond. / It's just because I've been at home with her. / Anyone can do it. / I am her mother.

*

You can pretend that you do not live in a city divided. People see what they want to see. They see what you want them to see.

Very early on, I felt that there was a choice to be made. I could give myself entirely to motherhood and relinquish my old life, my work, my friends, everything I had ever loved. Turn around and not look back.

Or, I could pretend. I could try to be what I wanted to be, and the woman they expected – a woman unchanged, a woman for whom childbearing was a blip, an event like all the other events, as big as a change of job, or a new home.

I longed for this to be so, never said that it was not.

What if we could be mothers and citizens of the great wide world? Not to be hidden away in our homes and our groups and our special cafés, our corners of the internet, corners of the park. What if mothers could remain people – everything we are; all of it?

And, just suppose, maternity leave was not about leaving?

Suppose, instead, we mothers remain; remain in the world we know, stop hiding ourselves away, and have our babies join us. Suppose it was no longer our secret, the toil and the pain and the love. If we could let our friends and families and colleagues and acquaintances and even strangers know what it is really like. Let them help us. Do all this together.

Imagine what it could be like, if, instead of leaving, we stayed.

Perfect

I can't say this to anyone else, but you, I'll tell: I have produced the perfect child.

At home, it's not so apparent. It's when we go out, to friends' houses, to drop-ins, and I see them, the other babies. Other babies with other names, like Henry and Nur and Saffron and Arlo. I have to hold them, sometimes, while their mothers pop to the loo, and they smell weird, they're sweaty, or clammy, too heavy or worryingly light; made of all the wrong stuff.

'Isn't he gorgeous?' I say, regarding the snotty little potato in the lap opposite, being tended to by a mother who, mysteriously, seems to think that her baby occupies the same league as mine. She knows my baby is better – she must, it's so obvious, was clear from the moment we entered the room. My baby is snotty too, all the babies are snotty, but the ooze on my baby's upper lip is more of a gloss, like icing on a fairy cake, delicate, delightful.

Many of the babies are older, larger, with huge skulls and vast faces, the hairlines of middle-aged men, and the middle-aged tummies, too. Some of them crawl, which seems an absurd way to move around when they could simply sit, like my baby, who is perfectly capable of summoning everything that is needed; hear the sweet dagger of that screech!

Some are embarrassingly, droolingly stupid. Look at the way *my* baby manoeuvres the blocks! The intelligence with which my baby considers those dextrous fingers, how the palm goes up, smacks straight into that surprised face. It appears to be an accident, but our eyes meet, and I laugh, and my baby laughs; it was for our amusement, after all. What a clown! Clever bubba.

And then there are the younger babies. Useless things, just lying there, vacant of gaze, blowing bubbles at the ceiling. Who could mistake those scrunched lumps for anything approaching the splendour in my arms, who is even now frowningly producing a poo? Their mothers do a good job of trying, and I collude with them; after all, they have to take these inferior creatures home, show them about to relatives, endure a lifetime with them, knowing all the while that my baby is out there, wowing the world.

Sometimes strangers stop me to look into the pram. 'Beautiful!' they say, and I'm pleased that my baby's glory is finally being trumpeted, until they start to talk of babies of their own, now fully grown, who've moved away and started families and don't call as much as they should, and I know that they, too, are mistaken. My baby would never do that.

My baby is the perfect age and the ideal size, and across the weeks and months this somehow remains the case, miracle child.

My baby is the very best baby in the entire history of the world.

And I chuckle at my foolishness, the extent of my indulgence; I roll my eyes.

But really, deep down, it is the truest thing that I have ever known.

The Garden of the Night

Every night at twenty past six, CBeebies shows *In the Night Garden*, one of this century's greatest works of art.

OK, I'm kidding, but not as much as you'd think. I look at Salvador Dali's melting dreamscapes and think, isn't this all a bit knowing? *In the Night Garden*, though, is so pure. The first chimes of the theme tune, the glimmer of each star. The lone figure of Igglepiggle in his boat, silhouetted against the sky. How he kindles his little light and takes to the ocean, as Derek Jacobi invites us to journey with him to the Garden of the Night.

A nation of children is soothed, rocked, lulled, loved, towards bath and bed. All except for my son, who bursts into terrified tears.

The other day I found an old note on my phone, a sleep diary from when my daughter was eight months old. Here is a typical entry:

8.45 pm fed to sleep
Awake midnight fed until 1am to sleep
Woke 1.06. Fed until 1.25, back to sleep

Woke 3.05 fed to sleep 3.45
5.30 woke fed to sleep
7 woke for the day

The timings are the broadest brushstrokes, and the picture of the night that they paint is pretty bad. What it doesn't convey, though, is the in-between.

The hulk of the sofa, the dark shapes of pillows, of the other person in the bed, of our baby in my arms. Inside the fridge, sunshine bright; the oblong of my phone screen; the dirty yellow street lamps. The luminous white glow, at once distant and near, suffusing the upstairs landing; has one of our lightbulbs gone wrong? Am I so tired I'm seeing things that are not really there? Wait – oh, yes. It's the moon.

Mutterings and stirrings, distant mewls like faraway sirens, which sometimes grow louder and louder, but equally, sometimes fade into nothing. The flood of adrenaline that rammed me upright in bed at the tiniest peep. Or, conversely, the very few times that sleep really overcame me, the fishhook of her cry jerking through my innards. Snuffles and flumps, the swiftly repositioned blanket that buys an extra twenty minutes. The tide of peace upon which the baby drifts away, a meniscus of silence cloaking every cough and creak. Sometimes, I even tried to think quietly.

Around this time, in the earliest days of my motherhood, there was a big rise in sleep tech. Everyone was wearing a Fitbit or using their phone to examine the efficiency of their nights. Not having any sleep of my own to analyse, I instead monitored that of our daughter.

Sleep, for her, never seemed that deep. Legs and arms tangled with the swaddling blanket, her mouth opening and closing so that I knew she was dreaming of milk. Her breath flickered, and so did her lashes. Sometimes, when I thought she was asleep, her eyes would open for no particular reason, her gaze unfocused, before she returned to wherever she really was.

We had a baby monitor, an egg-shaped device that conveyed every sigh back to us in surround sound. The internet had offered us video monitors, and even sensory pads that beeped if the baby stopped breathing, or stood up. There seemed no particular method of distinguishing between the two.

Their manufacturers knew what we were all afraid of: that while we slept, the baby would die. Why else were their products called names like Safe Sleep or Angelcare? We chose a relatively low-tech model, put her down on her back, and hoped that would be enough.

Each waking required judgement calls: feed and calm before she is properly conscious and perhaps bypass the crying entirely, or wait until she is undeniably, unhappily awake. And so what might, under more relaxed circumstances, have amounted to, say, four hours of sleep, was instead spent listening, waiting, planning and preparing. During the feeds themselves, wrestling with oxytocin and fatigue, I had, at times, to pinch and smack myself to try to stay awake.

Afterwards, my daughter may have been finally, tenuously, unconscious, but I still had to unclench, stretch my back, curled from breastfeeding, stagger through the dark to my bed, where I would lie in the dark, baffled as to why, now that sleep was finally possible – not just possible but essential – it had become impossible. Come daylight, that four hours stood not as time taken but rest I had frittered away.

The Garden of the Night. I thought it was a familiar place, somewhere I knew from working too late, or coming back from a party, or when lifted from my mattress by an occasional bout of insomnia.

But if I had been there before, it was as someone passing through. With its gates now closed behind me, every sunset became freighted with unease: will she sleep, will I, is this the night that will restore me or tip us all over the edge? I grew to fear the waning of the day, would have called the sun up again if I could; found myself looking out of the window, willing it to return.

Stripped of company, of coherent narrative, of any kind of structure, the Garden of the Night is where I found out what I am really made of. And what I am made of isn't great.

My body became a machine, lumbering, increasingly slow, a rusted crane. Its mechanisms groaned and clanked as I hoisted the baby, my bra, my breasts, up and down, up and down. Come 3 a.m. my nightshirt would be foul with milk and sweat and baby sick, my nerves and nipples raw. Sometimes, not too often, I would pause to consider the white-lace fantasies I'd nurtured before I'd had children. The thin skin of reality, how easily we are torn.

'Go to sleep,' we whispered, or said, or cajoled, or wept. 'Please, why don't you just go to sleep?'

When things became truly intolerable, as opposed to

the everyday sort of intolerable, when life was confirmed as properly mind-losingly scary, when I had said This Too Shall Pass so many times that the words no longer held any meaning, my husband and I attended a sleep seminar at our local baby drop-in.

The room was packed; clearly no one was getting any sleep in our part of town. A nice woman, somewhat flustered, was in charge, and began by asking each of us, in turn, why we were there. Oh, the stories. Of babies and toddlers and children who could only sleep when held, or rocked, or when drinking breastmilk or from a bottle, or when holding a specific teddy that had since been lost, or who never slept, not a wink, not ever.

We were still listening, transfixed (but yawning) by these desperate tales of woe an hour later. The seminar was scheduled to last an hour and a half.

The final woman to speak was better dressed than the rest of us, and her expression was cheerful. 'My daughter?' she said. 'I just put her down, and she's used to it. She just goes to sleep.'

No one said it, but my God, the atmosphere in that room, as twenty-four exhausted new parents silently roared, *THEN WHY ARE YOU HERE?*

We might have torn her limb from limb, if we hadn't all been so bloody tired.

This is the way to the Garden of the Night. Which route do we fancy?

There's 'Crying It Out', otherwise known as 'You May As Well Leave Your Baby On A Rock To Die And Maybe In Fact You Have'. This involves leaving one's (freshly changed and full-bellied) baby alone to cry. Eventually, the baby will sleep, or it'll be morning, or both, or neither, because everyone's gone mad and just one feed will make it stop, no one can bear this for even another second, no one should have to bear this, this is torture, sod it, I'm going in.

There's 'The Interval Method', otherwise known as 'Come Back In Every Five Minutes To Reassure Your Baby Until The Baby Falls Asleep But There Is A Decent Chance You Will Go In Every Five Minutes For An Entire Night And Everyone Will Be Crying By The End If Not The Middle And In Fact Why Not Start As You Will Inevitably Go On'.

Then there are various methods like 'Being A Silent Presence In A Chair That Moves Closer And Closer To The Door Until You've Left', which means sitting in rigid silence for many weeks while the baby reaches for you with desperate arms.

Tried co-sleeping? Bought a DockATot, a Snuggle Pod? Or, for just £130, a Sleepyhead Deluxe?

Or we could stick with what we know, i.e. 'No Sleep'?

Except that I

is she crying   does she need a feed
I can't even   my bones hurt
finish this sent—

I think maybe we should eat something is there anything no OK

Sorry.   What were we talking about?   Sleep?
Yeah, I do need to sort that.

And so we began.

*

Talking about this in public is like piloting a boat through shark-infested waters, tipping a bucket of chum off the bow and then deciding now is a good time for a swim. For those of us who find ourselves in the water, caught in the maelstrom of high emotion and vulnerability, unable to occupy our minds with anything else, it all gets very toxic, very quickly.

Sleep and sleep training occupy a section of baby – and child – rearing also colonised by feeding schedules and breastmilk and formula and so forth, all of which are things on which opinions are – and this is a substantial understatement – strong. I read that to deny my baby my breast or my arms was to abuse her, to abandon her, to damage her soul. I read that I should, in fact, be relishing these first precious months, which are over so quickly, after all. Something about this stuff – sleep, food, babies, their mothers – it drives people nuts.

Sleep, along with feeding, is one of the first junctures at which you can decide what kind of parent you will be. That said, such decisions, I found, are rather like the decisions one makes ahead of time about how one will give birth: interesting, and a useful exercise in taking ownership of what might otherwise be an alarming scenario, but not necessarily relevant to what eventually transpires.

Our baby will wake, we read. Our baby will cry. My husband will place a chair next to the cot and he will sit in it, a calm and steady presence. He may place a comforting hand onto the baby's chest. But he should not pick her up. She will be fine. And whatever happens, I must not go in to feed her.

To hear one's baby crying and know that you will not go to them is a very specific kind of hell. The books say that the response is physiological; blood pressure goes up, palms become clammy, the heart beats faster. For me, it seemed that my daughter's cries had the power to tear at the bonds of my being. My molecules rattled, and as her screams became louder and more desperate, I believed that I might fly apart.

I paced, dug my nails into the soft skin of my wrists, and then, when that wasn't enough, began to tear. I would have snapped off my fingers, torn my head from my neck and fed her upon my marrow. Anything to make her stop.

I must not go in. I could not go in.

I did not go in.

That first night of sleep training, the descent of silence took forty-five minutes. There was no relief even when, finally, the crying stopped. I pictured her, wide-eyed in the dark, stalked by nameless dreads. We had sent her out in her boat, way beyond the land, alone. She and I were not, as she had believed, one and the same. It was her first great betrayal, a second birth, and this time not into my arms, but to the cold embrace of an indifferent universe.

Well done us.

The next night it was agreed that all this weeping and rocking was not helpful: I had to leave the house.

It was late autumn, still warm. Our neighbourhood was busy and buzzy, restaurants lit up and full of happy people, in fancy clothes and jewellery, people who saw the night as a place for conversation and food and sex, a respite from the day rather than an ululating horrorscape.

After twenty minutes I texted my husband. 'Asleep?'

'Not yet,' came the reply. And then, even though I was half a mile away, I swear that I could hear her.

Night after night, I left my husband in the shouting darkness and walked and walked and walked. The images that played in my mind were relentlessly brutal: chicks, alone in their nests as eagles wheeled above; tiny monkeys, dropped to the forest floor, scuffling for animal warmth, their fingertips finding only leaves. Forty minutes of crying. Twenty-seven. Fifty-five. Eighteen minutes. Ten minutes. 'Tonight was fine. She went to sleep after six minutes,' my husband texted. 'You can come home.'

We'd done it. She'd done it. And still, it wasn't over. In teaching my daughter to settle herself, I somehow lost the ability myself, as though sleep were a baton that I had handed on. In the weeks that followed, as she drowsed, I would lie in bed exhausted, yet desperately awake.

And the light is so little.

To trust that at the other end of the darkness, there will be food and love and sunshine, trust us; it's a big ask, especially from someone who was only recently two cells, spread across two entirely different bodies.

My son, fed with a mixture of bottle and breastmilk, did not cry out so often in the night. When he did, my husband could go to him, and, as I was recovering from my C-section and then various C-section infections, he did, so that I could sleep and recover. I was grateful, quite wildly so, and yet, when he spoke of the night wakings, the jealousy hurt far more than my stitched-up abdomen. In those early days after birth my body seemed engaged in a kind of civil war: the need to rest versus the need to comfort my new and needy child. Once, very early on, when my husband told me to go back to bed, that they'd got this, he and my son, I retreated to the spare room and wept, hard, for an hour, before finally emerging to gasp out, 'I want . . . to feed . . . my baby.'

In those first weeks and months our son slept better than our daughter had, much, much better, and so we slept better, too. Which is just as well, we said to each other, and to others; with a four-year-old to look after as well as a newborn, and the operation to recover from, we need all the sleep we can get.

He fed so nicely. Not long, not deeply, the effort seemed to exhaust him, but he fed, and then he slept, and if we could not quite congratulate ourselves on the feeding side, so fraught with politics, then at least, we consoled ourselves, our little boy does sleep. See how well he sleeps, our little champion. Our little love. We're doing so much better, this time around.

He woke once a night, sometimes twice, and he stayed little, somehow; despite the passing of time, despite definitely growing, he seemed smaller and smaller still. By four months in, when night-time came, he was almost sleeping through.

'Well *done*,' everyone said, as we rose in the morning not quite refreshed – for we still had two very young children, after all – but not the zombies we had been in the first months of our daughter's life, either. 'Well done,' they said, and we said it to each other, too. Victory.

Or was it?

The stats from that time show his growth dropping off, as he drifted, then slid, down the weight chart, a feather falling, alighting at the bottom. And when I look back at photos of his first weeks and months, I see a baby verging on frailty.

Week after week, back to the clinic, the health visitor, the GP. No one quite knew what was happening, but one thing, at least, became clear: 'You have to get him out of the cot and feed him,' we were told.

'But, I thought, if he wasn't crying he was OK and . . . wouldn't he cry, if he needed to be fed?' I asked, hearing my voice, my certainty, crack. What I didn't say, and what I meant was, I thought that maybe, finally, we were doing well.

We looked down at my scrap of a baby.

'He should cry, but he's not,' said the health visitor. 'So you've got to do it. Wake him up.'

I thought again of our daughter's noisy tears; how vigorous they now seemed, how robust, the shriek of a soul whose grip on this world was entirely secure. And I thought of all those nights I had fattened myself upon sleep, blubbery in my bed, as my son, safe and snug, quietly starved.

Small wonder he still doesn't like watching Igglepiggle pilot his boat across the River Styx, and especially not at bedtime.

Now, my children sleep. Not always, not well, but they do, and it's only occasionally that we find ourselves back in the Garden of the Night, aiming the thermometer at an ever-moving forehead, squirting Calpol into the black shape that might just be a mouth, or sponging up a pool of semi-digested cheese and tomato pizza.

My body remembers, though, and I think my mind does, too. Get up at 4 a.m. for a flight? No problem. Deep sleep? Not really, not anymore. A few years ago, I heard a wonderful phrase, 'sleep architecture'. Yes! Sleep a cathedral, pillars of sleep, its soaring roof, spires touching the heavens. Before children, my sleep had a kind of majesty. Since, it's like looking at the Roman Forum – a pillar here, a collapsed lump of something there. Maybe half an arch. I can wander through, or look down and see what it once was. And it was awesome.

Perhaps it will get better. Later today we will take the bars off my son's cot, teach him to sleep in a big-boy bed like the big boy he is rapidly becoming. I know that, in the grand scheme of things, it's still early days.

But I suspect that I will always be listening, ready to tiptoe, or to leap, and gather them both in my arms. For a part of me, a large part, wishes still to stand quietly over their beds, just as I did on those first nights after they were born.

Wondering at the miracle of each inhalation, the quiet persistence of life. Thankful every second for the bright morning, all the mornings, still to come.

Buttons for Eyes

Right at the start of the pandemic, I killed our cat.

I mean, I didn't really kill him. But also, I did. Because he was old, and thin, and raggedy in the way that cats become. He was eating less and less and losing weight; he couldn't quite get up onto the sofa. I put a footstool in place, which he accepted, heaving up, once, twice, on legs that had lost their bounce. We both knew it was an in-dignity. When he harrumphed his way into his favourite spot, I did the decent thing and busied myself elsewhere.

Before he grew old, our cat was (with apologies to my daughter, who adores him still) an absolute bastard. Lying in wait in doorways to attack, not hesitating to draw blood if he thought it necessary, spending hours snoozing in a lap before exploding upwards in a volley of teeth and claws. When I brought my daughter home as a newborn, I caught him stalking her, once while she was in my arms. I was in the garden with a friend, who was holding a newborn of her own. 'Oh God,' she said, visibly alarmed, as we held our babies tight against the panther I'd allowed to share our home.

What could I do, though? If I'd taken him to the shelter,

he would never have found a new owner. Too ugly, too poorly, too vicious; he'd have sat miserably in a cage for a few weeks before being put to sleep. I can't *murder* him, I said to my friend. It wouldn't be right.

That's the problem with reading too many picture books, you see. In my head, all I could think was that 'Mummy Kills the Naughty Puss Cat' is not a story in which Mummy comes out well.

So, the cat stayed. Ultimately, it was age that mellowed him (I say mellowed, I mean broke). By the end, he was a scraggy, baggy old beast, puttering round the house, unable to bite with his poor sore teeth, too arthritic to scratch or stalk.

Anyway, come March 2020, it was clearly a matter of weeks if not days before he couldn't make it across the room, and, all of a sudden, this was time we did not have. That strange and terrible month, when we knew lockdown was looming and a net seemed to close over the world.

There was so much, back then, that we didn't know. Like, for instance, whether they would shut vets. Trying and failing to get a supermarket delivery slot, I wondered if we could really spend twelve weeks at home watching the cat's slow demise.

So I made the appointment for him to die the very next morning, desperate, heart fluttering, but outwardly calm, thankful that he couldn't understand what I was saying on the phone while my left hand absently fondled his ears. *I am killing the cat*, I thought. I am able, when it comes to it, to make the call, to coax him into a basket, to stay in the room when it happens. To watch.

Look, it was the right decision. The vet, visibly shocked when I tipped the cat onto the table, agreed, and then it was done, and I was at home with an empty carrier, trying to explain to a small and frightened girl that there would be no school on Monday, and no, she couldn't see her friends, and by the way, the cat has gone on a sort of holiday and I wasn't entirely sure when he would be back. Yes, it's weird, but see, we're all here, safe; CBeebies is playing, dinner's in the oven. No, we won't have the news on, not today, thank you, but, and, also, everything is fine.

A few years ago we inherited a paperback copy of *Coraline* by Neil Gaiman, a book so terrifying I knew at once that it could not stay in the house.

Coraline is a little girl who unlocks a strange wooden door in the corner of the drawing room to find another flat, the same as her own. In this place she meets her Other Mother.

Other Mother looks like Coraline's mother, sort of, only she is taller, much taller, has paper-white skin, and her long and curving fingers never stop moving. Still, she is kind and pleasant, and cooks roast chicken for lunch.

Coraline is delighted with her discovery and ready to embark upon a whole new life next door. The only snag, and it's a small thing, really, is that Other Mother has shiny black buttons instead of eyes.

This Other Mother was on my mind a few years ago back when my boy was small, maybe eight months old, on the morning that he and I went to Great Ormond Street Hospital. There we met a young consultant who spoke so sweetly and seriously to my baby that I loved him at once. Goodness knows I was ready to bestow my adoration, for my little one was too little, too thin, and we'd been passed from health visitor to GP, from GP to paediatrician, until, finally, we'd reached the last person; climbed, exhausted and gasping (in the baby's case, rather too literally), to stand here, at the pinnacle of NHS expertise.

'I need to see down his throat,' he said. 'I'll pass a tube down with a camera in it, up his nose and into his windpipe.'

'So . . . we make an appointment to come back?'

'No, come downstairs. We'll do it now.'

We went into the room. 'You have to hold him very firmly,' said the consultant, showing me how. 'He won't like it. Don't, whatever you do, let go.'

So I held my little boy very still, and told him that everything was OK while the doctor passed the tube up his nose and into his throat.

He didn't like it, and I did not let go.

We got the diagnosis the consultant had been hoping for, and I thanked him as we made our way back upstairs, the baby sobbing his tiny heart out all the while. Afterwards, as I ploughed the buggy back towards the Tube, he was still crying, twisting up and around to look at me.

Who are you? he seemed to be saying. *How could you?*

It's a law of parenting, unspoken but assumed: we must never let our children know the real horrors of the world. 'But Mummy, why can't I talk to strangers?' can never be answered with the truth, of course it can't. We teach them about danger: *hold my hand when we cross the road; stay close in a crowd; that's hot, WHICH IS WHY WE DON'T TOUCH IT.* My children fear my wrath far more than the impact of a car. We speak of being 'a bit lost' or 'nasty people' or 'getting squashed'. The danger is there, but never here. Always at a distance. Yes, it's out there, and it could get you, but it won't, because I won't let it.

They know fear, though. They know it just as well as we do. Perhaps even more, for they are closer to wherever it is that we pull ourselves from, that place, the cliff's edge. And while children may feel invulnerable, they are aware that they live in a world that was not built for them. Children know more than we think.

Have you ever seen a child having a night terror? It's scary as hell. In fact, the child might be *in* hell, or seeing it, or something, screaming or quietly weeping, inconsolable, unaware of touch, the room around them; eyes unfocused, hair messed with sweat. You're not supposed to wake them – indeed, the child probably won't be woken – so you just sit and pat and speak calmly and quietly and hope that whatever beast has your beloved in its hot jaws will quieten, too.

It's strange, knowing that your words won't soothe, can't even be heard. Sometimes, when my daughter cried, I thought that rather than helping her, I was calming myself. But you have to say something, don't you? Just like I had to say something to the poor cat, on that high table, his pink nose filled with the smell of disinfectant, as the world around him faded away.

'She didn't mean it.'

'We're nearly there.'

'You won't feel a thing.'

Oh, we're all Other Mother, every one of us. Exposing a plump arm to the needle. Tipping the weeping two-year-old into the arms of the nursery assistant. Sending the child back up to the shadowed bedroom – *yes, I know you can't sleep, but you've come down three times now and I don't think you've even tried.*

It's an interesting, if disturbing discovery of parent-hood, that things can simultaneously be fine and also not.

Very few of the world's baddies would think of them-selves as such. However hideous the atrocity, there's pretty much always some justification. And what could be more terrible, when you are only a few months old, for the person you thought would never hurt you to be the one who tempts you onto her lap, holds you tight and close, and closer, and tighter, and tighter. I am afraid of Other Mother, even when Other Mother is who I am.

Then again, without Other Mother, there would be no independence, no vaccinations, no swift diagnosis by the kind doctor. Other Mother is vital. She gets shit done.

What they don't know, and what I must not tell them, is that my deceptions are as painful for me as they are for them. Being a traitor is hard: intellectualising is brittle armour in the face of a baby's terror.

It hurts us both, but they forget. Of their infant jabs, of that first morning at nursery, they have no memory; it's just me who replays these moments, over and over again.

Now, when I think of Other Mother, I wonder if she is OK, in her nightmare world just beyond that strange wooden door.

I hope someone finds her, smooths her hair, and maybe

sends her back to bed, just for a few hours. Takes out the buttons, which hurt. Puts them back into the tin beside her pillow. And holds her when, finally, in the quiet reaches of the night, she lets her eyes overflow.

Bumbo

'I thought we were bringing the Bugaboo.'

'You never said anything about the Bugaboo.'

'I did. I definitely said to bring the Bugaboo.'

Oh, the menace with which I could load that stupid word.

'If you'd said *Bugaboo*, I'd have brought the *Bugaboo*.'

Bugaboo, Sleepyhead, Grobag; my husband and I lob their syllables like grenades.

'Not that one. The one with the rainbows on it.'

'We always take the Tommee Tippee.'

'Where's the cunting Bumbo?'

When I had my first child, words – my words, words used for and about me – changed.

It was especially palpable right at the start, when the personality around whom all this revolves didn't even have language yet. Yet still, I found, everything was different now.

Round the corner of the department store or the supermarket, and there it is, the code that indicates this is for you. Want a sunshade for your buggy? The salesperson might show you something made by Dooky or Ickle Bubba. And when it comes to bedtime, you can choose between a Kutikai and a Shnuggle.

This is the language of new parenthood, new motherhood. No complicated syntax. No complicated anything, in fact: just sweetness and calm and fun. And that's OK, when I'm talking to the baby. Less so when other people are talking to me.

'And how's Mum?' they would say, at the clinic.

'I'm looking for something called . . . Windi Gas?' I would ask the chemist.

'Could it be the Baby Blues?' says the website.

On the maternity ward, at the drop-in groups, in Boots, it seemed that I had, on some linguistic level, *become* my baby. Is Mummy all right? Does she need her beddy-byes? Would she like a bickie? Perhaps I'm being hyperbolic, but it felt like the Newspeak from *Nineteen Eighty-Four*, designed to make wrongthink impossible.

For if we don't have the words to articulate the rage, the love–resentment, the pain–awe–fear, then maybe we won't feel them. We'll certainly find it harder to express them.

Which is helpful for everyone else, as they can carry on with their own lives uninterrupted. Carry on rolling their eyes as they skirt the woman standing in the middle of the pavement, her My Babiie Dreamiie holding a newborn that won't stop crying. Cut her maternity services. Sideline her in meetings. Sneer at her in the checkout queue and shout at her when she tries to manoeuvre her buggy onto the bus. Turn down her application to work four days a week and give half her job to the man who replaced her while she was on maternity leave. Harass her. Belittle her. Maybe make her redundant. Tell her she is wrong if she works and she is wrong if she stays at home.

Yes, something seems to be awry. But who cares when everything is dotted with daisies, comes from Izziwotnot, Seraphine, Turtledove?

In this 100 per cent pure cotton world, how can, indeed how *dare* a mother feel anything except Joie.

Part 3

Be That Woman

Me Time

I'm writing this in what remains of my lunch hour. Ten minutes of it were spent preparing and serving, five eating, and it's a sign of how desperate I am that right now time spent eating lunch feels like my lunch hour is going to waste. The door is locked, the handle rattled by small hands. Faces appear at the window, and press, hungrily, to the glass. They're like zombies, I say to myself, and then dismiss the image as absurd. But no, actually, it's not. They want my body. They want my *flesh*.

I let the blind down, and in a room that vibrates with the sound of my children, I try to snatch a moment of peace.

'Me time', they call it. I haven't had any, not really, not since the pandemic began, and not much before that. Kids don't respect boundaries. They can't see them, won't acknowledge their existence. Children are invaders, benign and beautiful, but invaders nonetheless. As far as they are concerned, every inch of me is theirs, and always has been. 'Don't worry too much about vitamins and things,' the doctor said, back when I was pregnant. 'The foetus will take what it needs first and so it's just you that'll suffer.' I think I nodded. I might even have said, 'Cool.'

And so, my stomach is jabbed, my hair is grabbed, fingers reach down my top and faces burrow into my crotch. And it's . . . fine, isn't it? If anyone else were doing this, literally anyone else, then I'd have cause for complaint. When it's your kids, though, you suck it up. Or spit it out, if that's more appropriate.

'I just want you with me forever all of the time,' said my daughter, draping herself across my torso as the thermostat registered 34 degrees. I'd said I was thinking of going for a bike ride, to try to get just a little time alone before the snap of elastic pulled me home, and she wept.

Truth be told, I want her, too. I want her with me, safe. I would like to carry her in my pocket, maybe even back in my womb if it meant she was happy. And — oh God — but I want space. I want to stand alone on a windswept plain. I want to wake in an empty house with a day stretching ahead that is entirely mine.

I want too much, I think.

Anyway, I can't have it. Last night at six, I stole upstairs for a twenty-minute lie-down, only to awaken to screams of 'He's wearing Mummy's pants as a hat!'

Lockdown. The word was so extreme just a few weeks ago, and now it's whatever the opposite of that is; I don't know because I can't think because there are always children, wherever I look, whatever I do, wherever I try to go. They give me everything, every laugh and every smile, and all their rage too (and the rage of a toddler is a terrible thing) and it fills me up. Not like a bucket, which can simply run over onto the floor; more like a skin, so that by the end of the day I'm swollen to bursting, my seams leaking their tears. And then there's the schoolwork to download and the clothes to wash and the blocks to put away and the resources to hunt down and I think that my mind is like the sitting-room floor: I can't see it because there's so much other stuff, stuff everywhere, and I can put it all away, but ten seconds later it's always, always back.

And then I think, one day, in ten years' time, maybe not even that, I will call them and they will not answer. The day ahead will be mine again. And all I will want is their laughing bodies, but when I reach for them, they'll flinch away.

I am inside out with love and rage and resentment and despair.

And now lunchtime is over, and my husband is calling me and when I go to open the door I find that it has been unlocked, all along.

High Wire

Despite their name, The Flying Wallendas do not actually fly. They walk, slowly, across an inch-thick high wire, above Times Square, Niagara Falls; once, above an active volcano. Sometimes they walk singly; often, in a human pyramid. They hold long poles for balance, making them resemble some impossible insect, feelers waving in the endless air.

They are a family of aerialists, the Wallendas, going back generations. The first, Karl Wallenda, debuted his act in 1928 in Madison Square Garden, with his brother and the woman who would become his wife. Their safety net had been lost in transit, so they performed without. (Oh, how I would love a transcript of the conversation in the dressing room before they went on.) The audience, of course, adored them, and their standing ovation cemented The Flying Wallendas as an act for whom a safety net has no place.

'Using a net has a tendency to make you practise less,' Tino Wallenda said recently, 'and you may be a little more daring than you should be.'

So, without their net, The Flying Wallendas take to the

high wire in a stack of seven people and – why not? – a chair. Doing headstands. Riding bikes.

And they fall. It is startling to see, written down, quite how many of them have plunged to eternal oblivion. There's fairly recent footage of an eight-person pyramid rehearsal attempt for the Guinness World Record ending in disaster. I watched a video of it on YouTube (checking first that no one died). What's striking is just how mundane it seems.

Of course they fell. What is extraordinary is that they ever stayed up.

The other day, I lay down for a nap in my daughter's bed. It was an event born entirely out of pragmatism: our bedroom was full of my husband, working from home, while the sofa was occupied by my daughter and various cuddly toys.

I'm tired, you see. Very tired. Because I can't sleep, and when I do, I have these dreams, silly dreams, clichés really, in which I am driving a car that is out of control, or trapped in a house that is falling down or going up in flames.

That particular morning, as every morning, I woke with a feeling of dread. It is as though I have a job interview in the afternoon, or an unpleasant medical procedure. It is like being filled by a swarm of bees. I open my eyes and lie still, let the bees land upon my innards, hope that they will fly away. Know that, held prisoner in the cavity of my chest, they never will.

This sensation first came upon me when I fell pregnant. I suspect it was conceived with my daughter and revealed itself, along with her, at my twelve-week scan, when my hormone readings were, apparently, wrong. To have failed so soon! And there was nothing I, or anyone, could do about it. 'I'm frightened,' I remember saying, and the person I told, a father, giving me a shrug. 'Get used to it,' he said, and I haven't, and I have.

To articulate what it is that I am afraid of is like pinning jelly. And when I do manage, my fears are so universal, so unoriginal, I wonder whether they are even worth stating: that my children or my husband will be unhappy, or sick, or both. That my husband and I will both become ill simultaneously, unable to cope. That it will all be too much and the children will die, or hate me, or be taken from me.

And then I think, yes, all of this, and, too, a fear of the continuing hard, hard work to stay simply as we are. Sometimes, often, the fear is of the fear itself; that the weight of it will break me apart, whatever bedrock there is of my strength eroding to collapse, the edifice that is me crumbling, parts shearing off piece by piece, until the whole lot gives way and spins down into the void.

The aerialist Philippe Petit once walked on a wire between the Twin Towers. No safety net for him! When the journalist Adam Higginbotham met him, he described him as 'incandescent with self-belief'.

But still, Petit is human. In his book *To Reach the Clouds*, he speaks of taming his animal fear, bit by bit. 'Oh! I am terrified . . . Yet I breathe in voluptuously the unknown that eddies below. I keep fighting.'

In Petit's case, I suppose, his is the fear of falling, a particular fear that is activated by the process of choosing to step onto the high wire. I, too, keep fighting. Indeed, my fight takes up a fair proportion of my every night and day.

Read Petit's book, though, and you'll find the whole endeavour is about preparation; dealing with every last eventuality. Guy ropes at precisely the correct tension, the integrity of the anchor points, clamps and U-bolts and knots and tape, minute calculations of temperature and wind speed – and all for that single foray, out and back. It appears to be a voyage into the unknown; in reality, it is anything but.

Petit will return to solid ground. That's the difference, I think. For me, there has been little in the way of preparation, and there is no way down.

For I have made my home on the wire. Sometimes, the wind drops and the sky is blue and I might even muster up a wave. But mostly, even as I wrestle one problem away, another is brewing. The rope beneath my feet slackens and sways and I think, if I knew the variables, if everything didn't keep changing, if the world could just stop, even for a minute, then maybe I too might be able to deem a safety net unnecessary.

Instead, I am afraid of falling, and I am afraid of staying up.

One foot, then another.

The sky is above and below, flickering with birds and unseen currents.

Keep going, keep moving.

Master it – the creature inside that says no; this small, furred, shivering thing that wants to run fast and away.

When I took my first steps out into space, the crowd

went *oooh*, and *aaah*. Then, soon enough, in ones and twos, they began to drift off. There are other acts, more splendid, more fantastical. Besides, I am no safety-net-less Wallenda, surely; I have enough to eat, a loving family, friends close by, the NHS. And it's just mothering, after all.

'I've known four people in my life either landed in a net or missed the net, and died,' Tino Wallenda has said. And when my daughter was around two, I felt my balance go.

Tell someone, they say. The books and the websites and the therapists. If it's getting too much, tell someone.

For a long time I assumed people knew.

They didn't know.

Finally, I managed to say, 'Help me?'

Nothing had changed; everything was as hard as it had always been, and everyone was so busy. People often talk of the friend you would ring at 3 a.m. All of us, I think, would take that call. But what of making it, and not at 3 a.m., but on a Sunday morning, when you know your friend will be in the middle of making lunch, or on the way back from football, or finally getting a well-deserved twenty minutes with a book, and you're going to ruin it by saying – what, exactly?

What, in the end, is there to say?

Still, at my husband's urging, I lit the distress flare, and then, in someone else's nice kitchen I said, 'I can't cope.'

My friend was kind. She said things like, 'You're doing better than you realise,' and, 'It'll get easier, just you wait.'

And that was it. Nothing changed.

What I was saying was that I couldn't even last another

day, that I was useless and hopeless, that I could not go on – I was saying all these things, and yet, of course, I was not. These emotions among new mothers are common enough that they simply do not register.

A few weeks ago, I texted my friend to ask what she recalls of that conversation. She had no memory of it whatsoever. For a moment, I was shocked; now, I think, well, why would she? For when things went wrong – properly wrong – for me, there were no words, or if there were, I could not imbue them with enough meaning.

It's hard, everyone knows it's hard, everyone accepts that it is hard. Are we too accepting, I wonder? We don't like it, and so we don't see it, or if we see, then we deny what is right in front of us. For to step back from the brink, to say, 'No, enough, I won't, I can't, things have to change because I can do no more' – it's simply not done. Especially not when there is enough money, enough health, when the house is warm and the children delightful.

Besides, I've glanced down. I know what's there. The endless hurt and tears and chaos and disappointment. The resulting trauma, generations of it.

Small wonder that I am so afraid. The standing ovations are generally reserved for those who make it to the other side.

It began with Karl Wallenda back in the Twenties. Now, seven generations later, I watch as, in a circus tent somewhere in the USA, a seven-person pyramid makes its slow way across thin air. They are all men, I think, all but the figure at the very top, seated on a chair. She is almost invisible; a part of the pyramid, yes, but one who appears to be doing no work at all.

Then, halfway across, she slowly gets to her feet and stands, and now she has all eyes upon her as she balances upon the chair upon the pole upon the two men upon the four men upon a single piece of metallic string. The crowd draws in its breath as one and I feel her sway. And then she sits back down, and the convoy moves on. The current Wallenda children are being taught the art of their parents. Soon, the internet assures me, they too will walk on wire.

When I lay down for a nap in my daughter's bed, I could hear the washing machine, the distant television; I could smell the chicken in the oven, my daughter's shampoo upon the pillow. Soon, I knew that someone would need me, call me, but right in that moment, it was enough for everyone simply that I was there.

For just a few minutes, there in my daughter's bed, I was a parent and I was a child. The sensation was curious, but not unpleasant. I was my own daughter. I was my own mother. I was both and I was neither. I simply was.

I heard the washing machine, the television. Smelled the dinner that I would eat, the child whose bed this was.

Soon, someone would call. But until then.

I closed my eyes. And I let go.

Filth

One cannot spend more than eight seconds in the company of a small child without getting dirty. Or them getting dirty.

Or both of you getting dirty.

Or you and them staying clean but the floor being flooded with milk, or piss, or . . . well, you take my point.

But *do you*? Do you *really*?

Because everything in my life is absolutely disgusting and you would not believe the amount of time and energy I am expending every bloody day trying to make this not so.

When I look back at my pregnancy photos − which I do, occasionally, you know, for a laugh − I see myself filled up with my daughter or son. Plump and flushed and encased in florals, there I am, gourd woman, sloshing about with limbs and waters, but all so neatly and entirely encased.

Pregnancy is the last time I can remember when I − everything − wasn't vile.

It starts when they come out. Newborns emerge slathered in whitish gunge, webbed with mucus and clumpy blood. My animal self didn't mind, perhaps because it was such a relief that the birth was over. But oh, when they give back the baby in all those pristine clothes you packed and now your child is clean, and you remember, or are reminded, or you see the world afresh.

The skin on a baby, or a child for that matter, after a swipe of damp kitchen roll, is somehow more pure and perfect than spring water. Reach out and touch it, your own fingers rough and gnarled.

And, ah, when they come out of the bath. The scent of them. The flushed cheeks, the only-just-unfolded pyjamas. Their nostrils are clear, their hair silkily free from cradle cap and pencil shavings and tomato sauce. Their hands, their fingernails, armpits and belly buttons. The weight of them as they climb onto my lap, and I surreptitiously push my hand under their clothes, to smooth their glowing backs, as we turn the pages of a bedtime story and nestle close.

The baby is clean. For all of eight seconds! And then . . .

How can these purest of creatures generate so much dirt? Not just generate it, but remain indifferent to it. 'Children don't see crumbs,' said a perceptive friend once, and he's right; until I was an adult, I never noticed if a carpet needed hoovering or when a hand towel was begging for a hot wash.

So, then. Filth. Where do we start, I wonder, standing with a box of wipes in one hand and the dustpan in the other, and the bath run and the kitchen counter readied with an array of products, each more toxic and abrasive than the last.

Where shall we begin?

Shit

Everyone knows about the shitty nappies. In fact, I have come to realise that shit is fine, when it is in a nappy. (It's not *quite* fine. It's shit.) It is when it escapes the Pampers that we have a problem.

Shit on the walls. Shit in my hair. Shit, more than once, in my mouth. Shit that lingers on my hands, somehow, despite six washes in increasingly hot water, each time with the baby left screaming next door; but, come on, I can't hold a baby, can't do anything, until that smell has gone.

The shit that, unnoticed, dribbles into the clothes so that the baby, smiling, cooing, has a warm yellow patch on her back, which you cannot leave but know that dealing with it will mean shit going everywhere, down the legs, across the changing table (usually someone else's), up the neck and into the hair.

The shit that is squeezed out right there in front of you, because you started changing the nappy too soon, so have no choice but to wait until it is done. It's as if you are watching a tube of toothpaste empty itself from the inside.

Shit in the washing machine, heated to 90°C: poo soup.

The woman rushing past at the play café, shouting, 'Get back! Get away!' and holding a tiny child entirely covered in shit, as though it had been dunked. (I still don't know what happened there and am quite glad that I will never find out.)

The shit released in the bath, prompting a rapid exodus of toys like that scene where everyone rushes out of the sea in *Jaws*.

Snot

How do children not know when their noses are snotty? Seriously, HOW DO THEY NOT KNOW?

My toddler comes, beaming, towards me, arms open and eyes wide, and all I can see are his two little nostrils stalactiting with snot. The sneeze that ejects a molten bogey thirty centimetres long. (I exaggerate, but not by much.) A rivulet down the top lip; the bright gleam of it on a winter's day.

'Come here,' I shout, brandishing my tissue, and he screams and runs; but no, I will not be the mother of the snotty child, I will not.

And then he is red and sore and there's still snot, more snot.

Rot

'There's something inside the bath toys,' says my daughter, peering into the little hole at the base of the rubber duck. 'Look.' She squeezes, and the jet of water that should be clear is flecked grey–black. When I hold up the thing to the light, I see that it is lined with mould. If one could somehow take away the rubber, there would be a perfect duck shape rendered in fungus.

Later, I remove every toy from the bathroom. Everything that gets wet, be it with bath water or saliva, is slimed with grey sludge. It's even inside Sophie la girafe; French sophistication is no barrier to these spores.

The fermenting nappies as you sit in the stuffy room next to the M&S loos, trying to breastfeed beside a bin that will not quite shut.

Down at the bottom of the toy box, there is a Thing. It is soft and sweet-smelling and a dark blackish brown. When I pick it up, using far too much kitchen roll, it is heavier than expected, and weeps a pale, pus-like substance. We eventually identify it as a banana, ancient and half eaten.

I think a lot about the cleansing properties of fire.

Scum

A miscellaneous category, this.

The ooze from Ella's Kitchen pouches that seeps into the car-seat straps and turns crusty. Sweet potato puree that attaches to the legs of the high chair, and the underside of the high chair, and the underside of the table (how? He can't even reach the table), which dries, sort of, into orange smears that won't come off without a scrape.

Play dough and salt dough and Pritt Stick and PVA glue. Cake mixture and icing and the packet mix for biscuits. Often, the whole lot together.

Whatever it is that has made the door handles so sticky.

The raisin embedded deep within a teddy bear's plush fur.

Old porridge.

Mud

'My baby brother has eated a mouthful of mud. Like a WORM!'

Crumbs

Includes sand and glitter and fleece fluff, and the exploded muffin and the inevitable fallout from toast.

Mainly, though, this is about rice cakes.

Rice cakes, which will more often than not pacify a whining child, at least for three minutes, and three minutes is ages. So everywhere you go, you have rice cakes ready, or being deployed, which means everywhere you go, there are crumbs.

Crumbs in the car. Crumbs down deep in the seams of the buggy. Crumbs on the sofa and around the sofa and in the sofa.

If you are feeling fragile, do not lift the cushions of the sofa.

Really.

Just don't.

Of course, I could just (deep breath) let it happen. Allow them to get dirty and me to get dirty and the house to fester, because isn't there something rather wholesome about that, in its way? They don't care. It's just me.

In fact, it goes beyond not caring: kids *actively want to wallow in gunge*. I had not heard of messy play until I encountered it when we went to look round a potential nursery for our daughter. In the baby room, a huge roll of paper had been unfurled and trays of paint laid out. The babies stood in it, crawled through it, lay down and rolled.

'Later, we'll get out paper shreds,' said the man giving us the tour. 'We do sand, water and outside there's a mud kitchen.' He paused, clearly sensing my dismay. 'We clean them up a bit before sending them home again. You'll need to provide spare clothes.'

Sand, mud, paint – and they were so happy, those babies, their small faces rapt with concentration, squishing the paint in lurid fistfuls, squelching it across the paper, plunging slick fingers into each other's mouths. They were having the time of their lives.

Maybe I dislike it because, really, I am the dirty one. I see all this stuff because I am filthy, with age and with experience. It's to do with sin, I suppose. And baptism. Tom the chimney sweep, in the batshit crazy Victorian nonsense that is *The Water Babies*, sagging gratefully into the river, saying, 'I must be clean, I must be clean.'

God, does everything have to be a metaphor? Stains can just be stains.

Yet still, I wash and rewash the sheets, then hang them in the sunshine, desperate to erase every last yellow smear.

Death will be clean, I suppose. Once the maggots have finished me off and I'm nothing but silence and bones. In the meantime I guess there's always sanitiser.

Health and Safety

My son has fallen down the stairs.

You draw the curtains and pull your children onto your lap, tell stories of the big bad wolf, of the wicked witch who locked the princess in a tower, and it's delicious, because at home you are together and you are safe. And then your son falls down the stairs.

It's not such a big deal, right? He's fine. A lot of screaming, a nosebleed, and within a quarter of an hour he's asking for a biscuit. Panic over. Back to normal.

But the stairs are still there. So is the knife drawer. And the kettle and the sockets and the pill packet. 'Roll them in mud,' says my aunt. My son eats mud, waddling out into the garden and scooping up furtive mouthfuls. I brush the crumbs from his cheeks and try not to think about the inner-city nature reserve we'll be visiting later, so full of broken glass that when the sun shines, the soil glitters.

When my daughter was around eight weeks old, I went to a talk on baby health and safety. I'd assumed, as far as I'd thought about it at all, that it would be routine, workaday.

We were welcomed in by the doctor, who cooed over our little ones as he shut the door.

That man had seen a lot of dead babies. Babies who chewed pretty dishwasher tablets, who reached into toilets and placed gel fresheners into their curious mouths. Babies whose faces were scalded when their mothers passed freshly made tea over their heads and the mug slipped from exhausted hands. The babies whose very same mothers ran to grab a bag of frozen peas, which they held to burnt heads, then lifted it away, and with it their babies' skin. 'Scalped,' said the doctor, with something not unlike relish, as we sat, knees jiggling our own babies, veins throbbing and mouths slack.

Babies with temperatures that soared, quietly, in the far reaches of the night. Babies whose rashes never quite matched those in the textbooks and Google searches, but who succumbed to meningitis nonetheless. Babies who simply stopped breathing. There was one, only recently, in our local park, the doctor told us, brought back to life by another mother who had known that something was not right, who pulled the baby from her friend's buggy and gave it mouth-to-mouth, right there on the spot. 'Be that woman,' said the doctor, and I knew instinctively that I would not. I'd be the buggy pusher whose baby would depart, unnoticed, while I pondered whether to nip to Tesco.

'I don't give them sausages, ever,' said my friend Harriet, when I told her. 'Not after Leo choked.'

'She wasn't breathing,' said Joy, a GP. 'It was just a grape and I'd cut it in half like you're supposed to. Her dad tipped her upside down and smacked her back and she coughed it up. But her expression . . .'

'He can't eat peanuts,' said Nat. 'If he has something that's even touched a peanut, been near a peanut, then . . .'

Leanne, a no-nonsense scientist, recounted how she'd nearly left her baby on a train; the doors had begun to close as she was turning back to take the buggy's handles. She'd screamed and someone heard and the doors had reopened and it had been fine. 'But what if it hadn't?' she said to me. The answer being, of course, that she and her baby would have been reunited half an hour later. But that wasn't what either of us were thinking. We both saw the other thing, the nameless thing, looked briefly into the face of the nightmare, turned hurriedly away.

Maybe it's a phone call. That's how it was for us. It happened when my daughter was still small, almost unbearably so, but my husband was out at work, and she was – surely – old enough to be watched by someone else for a few minutes.

It was a call I had to make, a call about a book, a potential route out of maternity leave and into the world of work; it was important. We were at home with a trusted friend. I would be upstairs, he would be in the living room and my daughter would be napping; I'd scheduled it for the one segment of the day that was my own.

It was a time I knew well, because I used it to do everything that could not be done while holding a baby. Washing, tidying, preparing and eating food, reading, thinking clearly, making lists, ticking things off from lists, sleeping, stretching, making and drinking tea, loading the dishwasher, putting water in the ice-cube tray (we were in the midst of a heatwave), finding and assembling the fan (again, the heatwave), examining my daughter's clothes to see what she had outgrown and what needed to be purchased or unearthed from our bag of hand-me-downs, wiping the changing table, devising some kind of plan for what we were going to have for dinner that night, going into the garden to breathe and enjoy the sense that my body was, for a few moments, my own. I had forty minutes.

Putting all else to one side (not easy, but it had been put to one side for the last few months, after all) forty minutes was plenty. Forty minutes to make a single phone call was *luxurious*.

My daughter had been nursing for hours. She had been jiggled and bounced and spent a somewhat psychedelic session examining the various textures of her play mat. Her nap was reliable, especially given the exemplary morning we'd spent together. The nap was a given. Was supposed to be a given.

The expansion of my horizon beyond motherhood's immediate sphere was both exhilarating and disquieting, and my restlessness must have transmitted itself to her, in the pitch of my voice, the scent of my neck, down through the cadence of the buggy as I pushed her through the park, back towards the house and then round the block, around and around. I had to make an important call.

Of course she couldn't sleep. How could she?

Back home, we tried again. There was rocking, singing, and when I lay her down in her cot, a long and outraged scream. Perhaps she was still hungry, I reasoned to my friend, who gave me the blank smile of one who has no idea but is prepared to sit quietly until the rhetorical questions have finished. It's so hard to tell, I gabbled, because when you're breastfeeding, you never know how much has gone in, do you? He agreed, with the caveat that he had neither a baby nor breasts.

I prepared a bottle of powdered milk, the same milk she'd drunk the weekend before, and she took it, eyes wide. The time for the call drew closer, and eventually, I gave her to my friend to hold. She was swathed in a green muslin, wriggling and smiling.

Scan the scene once more, as mothers do. The wakeful baby. The muslin. The trusted friend.

'It's fine,' I told him. 'I'll just be upstairs.'

At that time, new to motherhood, I was still in shock; the things which previously absorbed me (books, the news, talking about other people, talking about myself) had been stripped away entirely, and any effort on my part to reinstate them would feel nauseatingly self-indulgent, as though a meteor were about to strike and in response, I had decided to learn the kazoo. Much of the phone conversation was therefore taken up with my exclamations of guilt for making the phone call in the first place, which probably lengthened it by about a third. But for a good fifteen minutes, I discussed my work, made a plan; felt like myself. For that intoxicating quarter of an hour, I was able to give the whole of my mind over to a single task. It was the first time I had done so since I had given birth to my daughter, and it was wonderful. As I came back down the stairs, arms out to receive her, I almost danced.

'She's been sick,' confessed my friend.

'You mean posseting?' I said, enjoying using a word which spoke so prettily of the nursery, of wicker Moses baskets and embroidered cotton.

In fact, it was much more than the dribbled slime of posset – a warm, white lapful. I apologised, we laughed, and I picked up my baby and gave her a squeeze. In that moment, reunited, flushed with the joy of being both myself and her mum, I caught a glimpse of contentment, the clouds parting to reveal a single sunbeam bathing us both in light.

She was sick again. Evidently she'd emptied the majority of her stomach's contents onto my friend's sweater; still, there was enough, this time, that we would both have to change. I held her to my shoulder, gave a showy sigh, and went upstairs. On the changing table, I pulled her dress up over her hair and she caught my gaze with that searching expression that babies have, her small mouth pursed, blue eyes round and interested, and then, in the next moment, alarmed. Under my hand, I felt her abdomen go rigid. She was sick, again. About an egg cup's worth of yellow liquid ran down the table and onto my legs. Bile. She was vomiting – and my mind had gone from posset to sick to vomit – though there was no milk left inside. Even to my exceptionally untrained eye, this was wrong.

The fear that had basked just below the surface ever since I'd fallen pregnant now came roaring up as I placed one hand on her chest, and with the other rang my GP. How old was she? I heard the receptionist turn away from the phone, a muffled conversation with whoever was at her side. Yes, they'd fit her in when surgery finished at six, in an hour and a half's time. Just get her dressed, maybe offer her a feed in the meantime to combat dehydration.

'See? Nothing to worry about,' I said to my daughter, as though repeating something I had been told, even though in fact, no one had said anything of the kind. 'In an hour and a half, you will be safe.'

I looked at my baby, and as I watched, she was sick again. I was aware of her smallness; the largeness of the bottle teat I'd pushed into her mouth, the flail of her arms now as I lifted her and took her downstairs. 'Only an hour and a half and then we'll be in with the GP,' I said, as my friend wondered what was happening. Just a precaution. Probably, I said, hearing the chirrup of panic in my voice, by then it will all be over. One of those trips in which we all know I'm being overprotective, foolish. Silly mother, wasting NHS resources and time.

My daughter retched, hard, her torso solid, and when it stopped I noticed the pinkness receding from her cheeks. Her arms drooped and her head lolled back. Exhaustion? I said her name and she twitched. Was sick again.

'Call an ambulance?' I said to my friend. 'Please? Now?'

My daughter lay in my arms, eyes opening and closing, as I repeated the postcode. We waited. Her eyes closed and this time, when I said her name, she did not respond. Her face was white, maybe grey. 'Call again,' I said. 'Tell them they have to hurry.' I held my daughter close, feeling her chest rise and fall. Put my ear to her lips to feel the murmur of her breaths.

'They're coming,' said my friend, back on the phone. 'Five minutes.'

Keep breathing, I willed her. Keep breathing. You can do five minutes.

What did I think, as we waited? I know I thought about her name, as I said it over and over. I thought of all the times it would be spoken across her lifetime, strung them together like beads. The wonder of her when she was newly born, the way we uttered it like a holy thing.

I am not sure whether I thought, then, she was going to die, but I think it now and I say her name to myself, quietly, as I write.

I was already at the door as they came, two men who bore my daughter to the sofa, lifting away her clothes to touch her chest.

'Look,' said the first, as he pinched my daughter's skin. 'It's white, and then,' he pinched again, 'the blood's flowing back? That's what we like to see. Her heart's fine, her oxygen levels are fine. We just need her to open her eyes.'

Even as he spoke, she roused a little and attempted to be sick.

'And hello to you too,' said the paramedic, and with that joke, I understood that whatever the danger was, it might have passed, or at the very least loosed its talons long enough for us to try to smile. 'So,' he said. 'Tell me what happened.'

That spring, when the house was draped in sour muslins and sleep was something for other people, we were summoned to our nearest health clinic, given biscuits and asked to watch a DVD. 'It's less than ten minutes,' we were told. 'Just a short film about crying.' And it was. Mums and dads, whose fresh faces and clean clothes told me that they were a good few months ahead of us on the road of parenthood, talked of bringing their newborns home, how wonderful it had been, how terrifying. Their words were interspersed with shots of screaming babies, as their parents, who were so in love with their offspring, so delighted by them, told us how bewildered they had been when, nappy changed, tummy full, cuddles given, their babies continued to cry, and cry, and cry.

The film's darkness filtered in slowly, and then all at once, like the ending of the day (although do days ever truly end when you have a newborn?) as the narrative hurtled from happy parents to exhausted parents to a cautionary health visitor to a calm paediatric consultant, until, at around four minutes in, we came to the point, which was: don't shake your baby.

To illustrate this, a computer-generated newborn's head was thrown backwards and forwards, and computer-generated blood vessels burst. 'It's really important to remember it's never your baby's fault, they're never trying to upset you,' the health visitor on the screen said. And then the babies settled as their parents smiled, and told us how they'd taken a break, sung 'Twinkle, Twinkle, Little Star', gone for a walk in the fresh air. The woman in charge of the DVD player passed around a second plate of biscuits. Of course none of *us* would ever hurt our babies, would we?

I did not stay to chat, but raced home, misted with sweat.

There is nothing so urgent and so unbearable as a distressed baby, as your distressed baby. What does she want? we asked, in those earliest days. Tell us what she wants, we begged the midwives, the doctors, our parents, each other. The need in those cries was fathomless. Please, won't someone just tell us what she needs? The answer was inevitably the same: 'You. That's all.' By you, they meant me. And by all, they meant all. Give her all of you. It was like being in a fairy story: give her your skin, your blood, give her your brain and your heart.

Certainly, she had my body. My belly was large and soft, my breasts primed for her call. She had my time. Tasks that I once would have considered easy, like rinsing a mug or finishing a sentence, lay abandoned for hours at the merest hint of a summons.

And she had my mind. There was the continuous spooling of immediate needs anticipated and met, the triaging of tasks between me and my husband. Our daughter was the nexus of every conversation, until I longed to talk about something – anything – else. 'Syria!' I said, to my husband, absurdly. 'Why can't we talk about the situation in Syria?' Not that I'd ever been one for talking about global politics. Besides, I'd spent the last month entirely occupied with having a baby. Whatever had previously constituted the line of communication between me and the outside world was lost. I hadn't stopped to think about it, had not thought to capture it, and now it was gone. And I had cared before, I had been afraid before, but this thrum was constant; it was molecular, it was as if, at the moment of conception, a string within me had been plucked, and from now until my death I would reverberate with *her*. The baby the baby the baby.

Those, then, were the thoughts that lay within my control. Then there were those that prowled the edges of my consciousness. When the wailing got too loud, the nights too long, when I forgot to eat, or sometimes for no discernible reason, they would rise, unfurling to impossible heights. I would imagine cradling my daughter against my chest, and then hurling her from the window. I could almost see the brokenness of her body on the stone below. Holding her head down in the bath, the expression in her eyes as her fingers clawed the water. Sometimes I would see myself place a pillow over her screaming face, watching, impassive, until the waving of her legs slowed and fell still.

I didn't want to hurt my baby, of course I didn't. Every cell of my being was working harder than I thought possible to keep her happy and safe. So why did my mind keep showing me these images? And where had I been keeping them? For my brain to have generated these thoughts seemed to make my claim to motherhood profane; in creating them, I felt tainted to the core. In my mind, I was killing my daughter, over and over. And no, it wasn't real, but so what? Reality, in those early weeks, dripped like hot plastic. Anyway, if I was capable of engendering such impulses then the doing seemed almost the lesser act.

Many years later I was told that such images have a name, that they are normal, and that they are, in fact, a mechanism to keep the baby safe. 'Intrusive thoughts', they're called, and damn right they're intrusive, tiger after tiger showing up for tea. 'Ninety per cent of parents have this experience', said one website, breezily. I look at women in the playground, at the library, on the bus, and think, really? Ninety per cent of you have imagined holding your baby under the hot tap? Is that what motherhood is?

And then it occurs to me that despite all this, no one

thinks they are really going to harm their baby, until they do.

As the paramedic held my daughter in his arms, I saw him scanning the room as he spoke, taking in the muslin, the milk, my trusted friend; all irrelevant. 'I don't know what happened,' I told him, although I did. What happened then, whatever happens, it was, will, always, somehow, be my fault. If I had not made the phone call. If I had not given her the bottle. If I had not gone up the stairs and shut the fucking door.

And now my son has fallen down the stairs and twenty-four hours later I'm still replaying it. Hearing the thick, heavy thumps, irregularly spaced, something soft turning over and over, hitting not every step but some here, some there, the gaps between thumps at first spaced wide, then less so, as the fall picked up speed. The silence, and the small sprawl of his body at the bottom.

What I know is this: I must be a shield and a force field, a many-armed god. I want – I have – to be safety itself. I understand that for my children to know freedom, they must know pain. Yet if I could wave the wand that meant he would never cry again, I would.

His nose is bleeding and I hold him: *Shush shush shush, you're safe, you're OK, it's all OK.* (It's not OK, that's a hell of a lot of blood – has he bitten through his lip? His tongue? Are his feet moving? And his hands? And why did I not shut the stair gate, why, why?) *Shush now, what would you like, my darling? Don't cry, it's all OK.* Parading the things he loves most, forbidden things, the TV remote, a pack of wipes – *Press the button? Take as many as you like!* – but he doesn't want them, of course he doesn't, he just fell maybe five metres? Sponging the blood from his dear wailing face and I'm vibrating with the shock of it, and I'm not surprised at all.

Because it's always there, sliding and stalking between the rooms, jumping from shadow to shadow. My children will be eating their dinner, laughing, and I'm almost overwhelmed with the urge to – what? – scoop them up and away to the safe place that doesn't exist.

'The princess can't stay in the tower,' says my daughter. 'She's got to come out. In the end.'

'What if she falls on the way down?' I say. 'What if the prince is mean? Or she gets eaten by the wolf? What if her mummy misses her?'

But my daughter has wandered off and grabbed a toy from her brother, who lunges to take it back and hits his head on the corner of the table. A corner that should be covered with a piece of plastic foam, only he pulled it off two days ago and I never quite got round to sticking it back on.

Hush now, my darling. Please don't cry. It'll be OK. Come here. You're safe. You're safe, you're OK. Come here. You're safe.

Maths

Please complete the following set of questions. You have until the baby wakes.

1. Five little ducks went swimming one day, over the hills and far away. Mummy duck said quack, quack, quack, quack, but only four little ducks came back.

What the hell happened to the missing duck?

2. During labour, Kate is asked by the midwife to rate her pain on a scale of 1 to 10. What frame of reference should she employ?

a) Root canal.

b) A broken bone.

c) It doesn't matter because she is only 2cm dilated and they're going to send her home anyway.

3. Estelle and Dev are unable to conceive naturally. They do not qualify for NHS fertility treatment. A round of IVF at their preferred clinic costs £4,500. After how many unsuccessful rounds should they call it quits?

4. Leonie (39) has been seeing Andrew (41) for eighteen months. Leonie would definitely like to have one child, ideally two or three. Andrew is unsure whether he wants to have children full stop and has asked for a year to think about it. What should Leonie do?

5. It is 5.45 a.m. and Tasha's son has woken with a cold:

Scenario a: He has a temperature of 37.4°C. Under nursery rules he is fit and healthy, and is allowed in for a day of childcare, which will cost Tasha £80. Tasha goes into work, where she earns £85.

Scenario b: Tasha's son has a temperature of 37.5°C. He is not allowed to go to nursery. Tasha is unable to earn £85 but still has to pay £80 for her son's unused place.

Scenario c: Tasha's son has a temperature of 38.6°C. Tasha is paying £80 for an unused nursery place, and she has been 'let go' from work.

Does Tasha seem at all stressed to you?

6. It is 8 a.m. You play peek-a-boo with your toddler for 6 hours. It is now 8.02 a.m. Explain.

7. Hold these numbers in your head simultaneously:

5ml Calpol 4 times in 24 hours but 2.5ml Nurofen no more than 3, 60°C wash, factor 50 sun cream, 4 inset days, 6 weeks of summer holiday, 100 CPR compressions per minute, vaccinations at 8 weeks, 12 weeks, 16 weeks, 1 year, 3 years and 4 months (there will be no reminders), ballet is on Tuesdays at 4 and Rainbows is on Thursdays at 6, parents evening is 7.55 to 8 p.m., late pick-up incurs a fine of 50p per minute for the first 10 minutes then £1 for every minute thereafter.

All figures are subject to change.

8. Like 79 per cent of UK companies, Ava's offers an enhanced maternity pay package. Her partner Oliver does not work for one of the 21 per cent of companies that offers paternity leave beyond the first two weeks. He can only take statutory parental leave. In their case, the difference between the two is £1,800 per month.

Why is it that Oliver does not stay at home with the baby? Please give your answer in the form of a national newspaper column containing the phrases, 'modern masculinity', 'office politics' and 'there are no easy answers'.

9. Estimates suggest that 1 in 8 pregnancies will end in a miscarriage, while 1 in 200 pregnancies ends in stillbirth.
   a) How many people do you know who have experienced one, or both?
   b) How many conversations have you had with them about it?
   c) Express answers a) and b) as a ratio.

10. Put a number on the love.

Part 4

The Book of Mummy

Hand-Me-Downs

'There was an assembly today, Mummy, and it was about people like me.'

I was in the middle of making tea, so not listening as attentively as I would have liked. Then again, it's hard to be entirely and constantly engaged, when the conversation can range from the endangered status of the ring-tailed lemur to 'Why did Ethan make a face at me in the lunch queue?' to 'What is the point of eyebrows?' and back to lemurs again, all while you're ransacking the freezer for a half-remembered box of potato waffles.

'There were these people, lots, and they were killed, and they were Jewish . . .'

And I retreated from the peas and sweetcorn and crumbs of breaded fish to confirm that, yes, my five-year-old daughter was telling me about the Holocaust.

It occurred to me, as she spoke – 'They killed them for being Jewish. And I'm Jewish!' – that this was something I probably ought to have foreseen. Yes, I really should have known this was coming.

And in the most abstract of senses, I suppose I did. The information, while unassembled, was all there, had always been there; if I ever had a child, that child would one day learn that, in recent history, a sizeable segment of Europe attempted to exterminate her race. I could have outlined a conversation with a shocked teenager: *Yes, us. Yes, you.*

Or, I might have mused, maybe it's best to start early, make it something the child always knows. So that she never remembers the precise moment of finding out that, historically speaking, a not-small segment of humanity has always wanted to see her, her ancestors, her unborn children, eliminated. The sky is blue, gravity makes things fall and people hate Jews.

So I did know that this was on the cards, and yet, it was a shock. Which was something to reflect upon, later, as I attempted to compose a message to the headmaster.

'I hugely appreciate that you are educating the next generation in atrocities that so many dispute even occurred. Like you, I believe that the only way to ensure history is never repeated is to educate, even when it feels uncomfortable. We are in complete agreement, and, of course, I defer to your educational expertise. It's just that . . . she's five . . .'

Email abandoned, I returned to my daughter, to unicorn pyjamas and warm milk, to unbraid her hair. It was in the bath that the question finally came.

'But why do I have to be Jewish?'

'You're Jewish because Mummy and Daddy are Jewish, because our mummies and daddies are Jewish, and theirs were Jewish, too. And theirs, and theirs, and theirs.'

When my pregnancy was announced, there was a

collective gasp. Then, in great and gleeful exhalation, came the clothes.

'Take it,' friends and relatives cried, hauling bin bag after bin bag from the boot. 'Take it all.' Profoundly grateful though I was, I couldn't help but think of all that stuff and how it had sat, layered and compacted in lofts and garages, before it was finally extruded in heaps into our front room. Its former owners' delighted, dancing relief as they surveyed the new space in the car, suggested that, like me, they equated the disgorging of their hand-me-downs with a long-awaited and much-anticipated emptying of bowels.

The afternoon I finally opened the bags was disquieting. Huge with a very present baby, I dug through strata upon strata, excavating my future child's future wardrobe. Some of the clothes bore ghostly imprints of their previous occupants in the form of faint yellow stains around the neck or crotch. A few, which had managed to evade washing before they had been packed away, had something of the pressed flower about them, or an ancient cookery book speckled with crumbs.

All the outfits seemed vast, both in actual size and in what they represented; for me, at eight months pregnant, it was, in every sense, too much. Here, under my left hand, was the moving bump, and in my right, the babygro that would, one day very soon, be filled. Between the two, simply my skin. It was my first moment of feeling like a conduit between past and future. I washed and folded and washed and folded, burying everything once more, this time in the drawers of our new nursery, a roly-poly creature busying myself for winter.

Fast forward a few months, and those very same friends would invite us over at weekends for tea and biscuits, the careful socialising of new parents. The conversation was always the same – sleep and feeding, 'Is mat leave treating you OK?' and 'How is work?' – maybe an exchange of cake recipes, nothing too heartfelt or controversial; a tacit acknowledgement that right now all passion was very much spent.

Which is why I noticed when, confronted by my daughter wearing a particular cardigan, dress, or tiny socks, our hosts would crumple, actually crumple, with emotion.

'That's *ours*,' they would say, and it became apparent that their old clothes were irritants no longer, that they had become time machines wrought of polyester, cotton and wool. 'Remember Cleo in that?' Then, to us, 'She wore it at her cousin's birthday party, they had this crazy entertainer, he was so loud, and we were going to take her outside, but then she stood up on my lap and danced. And . . .' Eyes would flick between their child and our baby with all the astonishment of those gazing at the Grand Canyon, marvelling at who their girl had once been, and who she had become.

Poppering my daughter into her old–new wardrobe, memories of my own would resurface, of beloved corduroy, an underskirt scattered with embroidered flowers. 'What happened to those dungarees?' I would say to my mum. 'The bridesmaid's dress? That tartan jumper, you know, I wore it all the time.' As I spoke, my mind supplied not just the feel of it, the scratchy collar or the fuzziness of flannel, but my small limbs, narrow hips, nipples stretched flat across my chest. The pink clumsiness of my burning hands, bewildered by buttons, struggling with a zip.

On Sunday afternoons, we would load up the car, drive to our childhood homes, and while Grandma and Grandpa held the actual, current baby, my husband and I examined old photo albums with forensic interest.

Yes! There they were: the printed tunic that later flopped from the torso of my sister's doll, Big Baby; the smocked blouse. Some I only remembered from particular details, a section of crochet, the fringe of lace around a hem. Even my gaze was different then, I discovered. My memories had been acquired with the micro focus of babies and small children, who can spend whole minutes poring over the intricacies of a care label.

The past was what had led us to the albums; the outfits, our young parents, the gravy tint of the Eighties décor. We wanted, I suppose, to glance down the ladder, in these, our first visits back to our parental homes as parents ourselves. But if we came for the clothes, it was for the faces that we stayed.

'It's her,' we'd say, awestruck, looking at a particular snapshot of my six-week-old self.

Who knew, back then, that our daughter was already, somehow, present? Or, more miraculous still, there in the face of my grandmother, sepia no barrier to her toddler seriousness, balanced upon some distant relative's knee?

It's hard, looking through old family photos, when you've just had a baby.

While my grandma died younger than anyone would have liked, I think – hope – that she had a good life. Still, my heart twisted when I saw her so small and solemn. It might have been the weight of all that was to come, the sheer breadth and depth of it. It could just have been the expanse of time between then and now. Or was it that these photos showed me something I was striving to keep back; that one day, my fresh new child would be in the ground?

There is no single name for this very particular emotion, at least none that I can find, although there is the phrase that the Japanese love: 'mono no aware'. Translations throw up words such as 'bittersweet' and 'pathos', but the version I like best is literal: 'the aahness of things'. Cherry blossoms are the classic example: flowers that begin to fall even as they burst into bloom.

When the photo albums were back on the shelf, I looked at my daughter, sleeping in my arms. I imagined her unfurling, petal by petal, and thought, we are falling, you and I.

It's more than just faces, it's expressions, too. The slightly bashful quality to my husband's smile, even as a one-year-old. What appears to be aloofness in the interplay between the curve of my grandmother's nose and her heavily lidded eyes – something my daughter and I share, too – which is really a kind of masked nerviness, a prolonged intake of breath.

These faces are partly so compelling because we know, at least to an extent, what it is to inhabit them; they are our most personal furniture. Which inevitably makes me consider whether it's not just features and mannerisms that have been passed down, but the emotions that drive them, too. My grandmother was anxious. My mum is the same, and I, too, wrestle almost minute by minute with an internal octopus of imagined doom.

Last night, my daughter padded down the stairs to tell me that she couldn't sleep, and I recalled all the nights I spent as a child, listening to the fade of traffic, the slow quieting of the rooms below as my heart rate increased, aware that soon I would be the only person left awake in the house, in the world, and I said, and meant, more than she could yet understand, 'I know.'

Going into my twenties, it seemed to me important, urgent even, to get on with the business of independence, to put time and space between me and everyone I'd grown up with. The tall London house I shared was, in the right light, rather romantic, and my family, if I'd allowed them to get too close, might have pointed out that living off Tesco's 7p bread was not. They would have noticed that my room backed onto the main line out of Kings Cross and every time a train passed, which they did at a rate of around one every three minutes, my window rattled and the bed shook.

They might have pointed out that there was a crack den three doors down, that I was usually cold and often sad, that I didn't have a clue what I was doing. More to the point, they could have seen through this new me, the person I was trying so hard to become. Had I allowed them the opportunity, they might well have said that the life I was crafting was at best a piece of self-delusion, and at worst, insane.

So I tried not to think about them too much, all those people who loved me, who made me, for to do so would be to allow the past to tie me down, a million threads pulling me back to a place where I could not deny my dependency, would never truly be free. Sure, I would drop in on my family a few times a year for a bath and a hot meal, a traveller overnighting in a conveniently situated inn, before pushing forward and on. My past is a part of my life, I would think, but a small part. An appendage, not a foundation.

And then I had children and suddenly it was there.

Like an army, camouflaged in the trees. You thought that the clearing was empty – just you and distant birdsong – but no, it was watching and waiting, all along.

In vowing to be different from my parents, to lead a life that was truly my own, I had made the error of thinking that I was able to operate outside the forces that shape us all. That I was special. When I said to myself, 'I will be different,' I failed to factor in, you know, everything.

'When I am a mummy I will be a nice mummy,' I would say, with the particular furiousness that only a three-year-old can muster, retreating to my room after yet another row. It simply never occurred to me that when I was a mummy, I would have my own strong-willed, curly-haired little girl who would not go into the church hall for Stay and Play, no.

I look at the mothers now, and think, how could I not see you? All these years, my whole life, you were right there beside me, and I thought that I would be different, and I was wrong. In becoming a parent, it is as if my mum's interior world has been lit up for me, like that famous picture of Grand Central Station. For it's only now, as I experience the frustration, the bone-deep tiredness of it, the failure to argue logic to someone for whom logic does not yet exist, that I understand those fights that replay in my memory, my mind's eye down at knee level. And it turns out that I was squirrelling them away, bit by bit, each irritated shout shoved down deep in the far recesses of my interior.

Character, learned behaviour, genes, what we've observed consciously or not, parenting is like hefting around Mary Poppins's bag, and then, in the moment, reaching in and holding something aloft.

And so, standing outside the church hall, knowing that Stay and Play has begun and my daughter will not, for reasons I am unable to fathom, go in, I open my mouth and out it flies, so familiar it's embarrassing: 'We are going through that door. Because it's raining. Because we are late. Because. I. Said. So.' My mother's frustration turns out to have been packed up like one of those toy tents: touch the zip once and the whole thing pops up, complete, whether you wanted it there or not; and in that moment, I am not myself, at least, not entirely.

Which leads me to ask, just how many generations reverberate in this shout? Exactly how far back does it go? It is absurd to think of a mother outside a wattle and daub hut, draped in animal skins, snapping at her little one for rejecting an Iron Age playgroup. But I bet she bloody did.

'Be kind to yourself', the websites say, and I forget, sometimes, that every shout is outweighed by the quieter moments, whole minutes of honeyed joy. The slip of a nipple from a sleeping baby's slackened and sated mouth; the cuddle that soothes sobs to silence; 'Rock-a-bye Baby'; the discovery that, like my own mother, I always have a tissue. The slow smile that spread across my daughter's face when I first put her onto a swing and pushed. My little boy, going down our tiny slide and landing straight into the paddling pool I'd placed there on a sultry August afternoon, how he shrieked with pleasure.

Note to self: all this is motherhood, too.

I think back through all this with the sighing annoyance of a youngest sibling, whose buggy has always been crusted with years of others' snacks, whose coat bears three different name tags and is emphatically the wrong colour. I want to be me and I want my mother's life to be hers — not for both of us, all of us, to be locked into some pantomime re-enactment of triumphs and tragedies past. No more hand-me-downs.

For the truth I am only now facing, with some alarm, is that the moment I decided to have a baby, I lost control of my own narrative. We are moulded by our children, in so many ways. Recently I discovered that genes do not just run down the family tree, they also come up. Mothers contain traces of all the children they ever have, for the unborn shed DNA, which is reabsorbed into the mother's body back through the placenta. Indeed, given that foetal cells are released in high quantities during spontaneous abortions, mothers are remade by children who never took a breath. (But then, no one needed a geneticist to tell them that.)

The inescapable reality is that in having children, I have, at least to an extent, finished my own life's story; I have written its ending. I see the finger trace my name on the family tree, briefly, before moving on.

Sometimes, it's OK. Liberating, even, to be reminded of my insignificance.

Maybe I should surrender to the voices without and, far more insidious, within; to the constant chorus: 'If you really cared, you would give your whole self to them.' It's what my biology demands; it is what the universe expects. To hold my own ambitions and desires, to claim even the smallest pockets of time, is a fight – with them, the world, with myself.

I would die for my children, in a heartbeat and without question, I would die for them. I would do anything for them, and also, I just want a minute to myself, a second to breathe, a morning to think; to remember who I was, am, who I still can be.

'Mummy,' my daughter wails, every time I leave the house alone or shut the bedroom door. 'Mummy, Mummy, *Mummy*.'

All I can do, the only thing to stop myself spinning back – because I can feel my very blood turn in my veins when she calls me – is to acknowledge that even if, on some level, I believe that I should give it all up, everything, for her, I do not want her to give up anything, not one ounce of her beautiful self, not for anyone. Not even for a daughter of her own.

It's not enough to assuage the guilt, not completely. But it helps.

And help is something I need. For now I am the mother packing snacks that will not get eaten, zipping up coats, and complaining that no one will wear their gloves. In the playground, one damp afternoon when spring is promising more than it has yet managed to deliver, my daughter befriends some older girls, and it's only me that spots the tremor in her legs, that slight hesitation as they turn together and make for the biggest slide. The show of bravery she is putting on for these sophisticated seven-year-olds is so obviously not who she really is. At least, it's obvious to me.

'Are you sure about this?' I want to say. Then I remember the young woman in that tall London house, the rattle of those trains, and fall back into silence. Even if I did call out to her, I know she would pretend not to hear.

Who am I, anyway? Just a mother, watching her daughter go.

And now there is the baby, who is utterly unaware of any of this, thank goodness.

We, the mothers, may be old, but babies are, mercifully, so exquisitely new. In that first moment, when you take your newborn in your arms, that juxtaposition of one's cumulative humanity and the blank slate before you boggles the mind.

Babies just *are*. It's their greatness, especially in the moments of those first weeks when you feel maximally freighted with generational weight. We fret and moan and flounder and the baby exists, entirely itself, even as we peer into the cot, searching for resemblances, and in doing so, showing them their future, showing them ourselves.

Whenever I am tempted to think that I am my parents, I have to remember that, no, we are not the same. If nothing else, the life I was building back in my twenties has consequences that reverberate on; decisions I made then, to stay in the city even if it meant that while my world was big, the rooms would always be small; my politics, my friends, all this will inform two childhoods and more. And my daughter and I are not the same person, even if the occasional flash might suggest otherwise. It's just the light catching a particular facet, reflecting back. Yes, in the moment it might be dazzling, and yes, it could mean something. But it doesn't mean everything.

Even if my whole life, every atom of my existence, is a meal that has been reheated over and over and over again, I am still absolutely incapable of truly envisaging any of it until right at the moment when it occurs. The weary parent warning the pregnant woman, 'Get some time to yourself, while you can,' has been me, along with the pregnant woman, batting all this away with correct and heartfelt annoyance. I have both unwrapped hand-me-downs with awe and hurled them into the car boot with relief. Before I had my son, I could not envisage having any child except my daughter. She filled me up. There was no more time, no more energy, to give. More secretly, in my soul, it was my profound belief that there was no more love. Yes, I could have another child just like my daughter. But I had my daughter. I already had everything.

I am thinking of all this as my son waddles over, mouth twitching with amusement just as my lips have twitched when someone says something patently absurd. We're both laughing as I take him in my arms, letting him fill my embrace, marvelling at the very *himness* of him, a whole other person, so familiar, so new. He and his sister are unmistakably siblings, and yet he is completely himself. 'I didn't know that I could love you so much,' I say, or try to say, as he slides his fingers, and then his whole hand, into my mouth.

Perhaps I have no imagination at all.

The bath water is beginning to cool as I say to my daughter, 'You are lots of things, and being Jewish is just one of them. You can learn about it, if you want. And then you can choose what it means.'

It's a messy business, memory, legacy, whatever you want to call it, sands shifting over the course of a lifetime, across the centuries. The anxiety that plagues me now may well have been the driving force that led my great grandparents to abandon their lives in Poland and Russia back in the early 1900s and come to the UK, without which, the likelihood is, I would not be here.

What now, then, in this precise and particular moment? This junction of past and future, my daughter looking up at me, our gazes connecting in the electric now?

The best thing I can do is to carry it, all of it, everything I have been given and saddled with and gifted, and learn how to sift through it. To teach my children as best I can, to take what we need for this season, while it fits and the weather is still chilly. To know that as my children grow stronger, taller and more sure of themselves, I may weaken, but we all have so much of what we will need, there, waiting, ready. Not all of it will be right, or even helpful, but it's ours.

'OK,' says my daughter, nodding thoughtfully beneath her crown of bubbles, and it's her living, right here and right now, that answers my unspoken question about inheritance, all the shouldn'ts and shoulds, the arms that lift us up, along with the burdens sometimes too great to bear.

See, I say silently, to all those who would have us wiped from memory. Look, this, here is my victory. It's life. Our life.

And it goes on.

Some Discomfort

There is a small room off a busy corridor, and inside is a raised bed covered with a paper towel. You know the one.

Lie back and look at the squares of ceiling or, if you're lucky, the ancient mural on the wall. If you crane your head, you can see your bag, down on the floor, and on top of it, your jeans, neatly folded, along with your socks and knickers. The blind on the door is down and the bed is surrounded by swaying slats of a particular blue–grey. There is a faint smell of disinfectant, and alongside the computer monitor, keyboard and phone, there is a box of tissues, and another of latex gloves. Make yourself comfortable, and we'll begin.

I want to write about what having children has done to my body. My first instinct was to turn it into a funny story – you know the kind of thing, a fifteen-minute stand-up routine, where I piss myself in a Tesco Metro. I mean, it doesn't feel especially funny from the inside. But I have you, my audience, to consider, and I want you to keep reading.

I suppose I could make it gruesome, instead. Would that be better? Goodness knows, it's easy to shock, if that's what you want. Not the sort of thing that appeals to me personally, but *Saw* took $103 million at the box office, so . . .

The whole thing is such a turn-off, you see. It's hard to think of anything less appealing than someone's account of their trashed vagina. Strange, really, as entertainment-wise, there's no shortage of mutilated women. If it's bodies you're after, women's bodies, then turn on the TV any time after 9 p.m. and you'll find an array of sexy corpses. That said, the sexiness only works if the whole of the woman has been butchered. A functioning woman who has had an internal part of her damaged is deeply unsexy. From a consumer perspective, you don't know what you're going to get until she's been unwrapped. Like taking delivery of a faulty tumble dryer.

Then there's the vexed question of dignity. Absurd it may be, but I do aspire to elegance, to grace, the swish of spotless satin. The distaste of all this – I mean, it's my vagina, for God's sake, and I'm not sure the woman I've been taught to want to be *has* a vagina. If she does, her period blood is blue and tips neatly into the centre of a sanitary towel from some interior china jug.

Some of this, one can embrace with the zeal of feminism. Stretch marks, say. What a badge of honour they are, those fine, silvery, eminently Instagrammable lines that attest to the great power of the human body, tributaries flowing to the great mother river within. I have yet to see anyone proclaim their incontinence as a proud symbol of feminism. Or their uterine prolapse.

★

Women's Health.

It's invisible and mysterious, dark and damp, a hidden well shrouded with leaves. It's the middle of the forest on a hot and steaming day, the leaf pile thick and mouldering, moist knickers and soiled pads. The phrase 'feminine hygiene', with its implication that women's bodies are intrinsically foul. There are secretions here, sweat, whole spectrums of discharge. Spots of blood, mulch brown and poppy red. Women's Health is smears and speculums, caps and pessaries. Beige plastic slid across the table in an overheated cubicle. It is 'knock before entering'.

Sometimes Women's Health is an internet forum. Sometimes a Facebook group, or a list of names on WhatsApp. Often it's a clinic. There are few men, here. Their lesson was taught back at school, when the time came to discuss tampons, and the boys were ushered away. Maybe that's why spunk is cool. Not cool like, say, a gun, but infinitely more acceptable than cervical mucus.

Think vulvas and perineums. Terms like 'lubrication' and 'elasticity' and 'flow'. Imagine saying these words out loud in a public space. The embarrassment is exquisite.

So I keep my problems for Women's Health, where the waiting rooms are crowded and the appointments are scarce. 'We release our coil slots once a month,' a receptionist told me. 'They go in about fifteen minutes. So set a timer on your phone and ring at nine on the dot.' It was not unlike trying to secure tickets for Glastonbury.

Even here, it's not pleasant, to speak of these things. This is no place for anger or despair. Anything beyond amiable compliance looks like ingratitude. How many children did you say you had, again? And how old? Lovely.

For infertility, there might be a doctor who responds with, 'Just relax,' or, 'Stop trying and book a holiday,' or 'You're very young/a bit old,' or, 'It can take two years, you know,' and, to a friend of mine, 'Have you thought about being grateful for what you have?' For fertility, the nurse who once, when I asked for a repeat prescription of the contraceptive pill, refused to give it to me because 'You might be lying.' I learned, fast, in Women's Health. While I don't have to get my husband's signature for my credit card or mortgage application, I still have to go to the doctor, cap in hand, obedient, nice, to ensure I don't have to hassle for another appointment, this time for an abortion.

Then there's the ultimate unmentionable, women's pain. The tears and the cramps. The grunt as the coil goes in. It is the moan as the midwife performs a sweep; the crunched face, open legs. Cries that are soft and stifled, even as they emerge.

Sit nicely, I discovered, and smile, at your relatives and friends, at the doctor who said, pleasantly, that the pain I experienced when I tried to have sex eighteen months on from the birth of my daughter 'wasn't something of concern'.

Don't bring it up, not in public, and certainly not over dinner. And anyway, does it really matter, this pain, this shame, this sense that year by year, my body is failing, crumbling, diminishing in value, when I have two such beautiful children, and how old are they, by the way, two girls did you say, ah, a girl and a boy? Oh, wonderful, now, just try to relax.

★

With the onset of my first period I discovered that when it comes to women's pain, the rules are different. Until then, pain had been something that I could hold aloft – *look, I cut my finger* – sure in the knowledge that I would find plasters and sympathy. Until I awoke one morning, my abdomen grinding and blood on the sheets to find that nothing, and everything, had changed.

No, I still had to go to school. It would be weird to mention on the bus that I thought I might pass out. If I couldn't wait until break to change my sanitary towel, I had to be sure to stuff the fresh one up my sleeve. No one wanted to know that I was bleeding and cramping. Really, when it comes to bleeding and cramping, no one ever wants to know. Hardly surprising, then, that in the UK the average endometriosis diagnosis takes seven and a half years.

This revelation paved the way for the next – the one that came in pregnancy, the one that everyone sort of knows but only becomes pertinent when there is a child inside that must come out; a particularly frightening game of What's The Time, Mr Wolf?

There will be pain. And, in a further shift from everything I'd ever known, everything that my body had understood, pain in labour isn't bad, it's good. It's healthy and helpful, something I, as a woman, must welcome and embrace.

It was like knowing that one day gravity would reverse itself. For nine months, I tried to prepare for something completely abstract; something that I knew, soon, would be so specific to me, this event, bearing down, the pain of labour which would be mine.

As is almost universally advised, I bought a fitness ball, an enormous thing that echoed my equally enormous belly. And I took an antenatal class, where I was told that an epidural could set off a whole chain of events, which, if I was brave enough, strong enough, relaxed enough, accepting enough, it was within my power to avoid. Trust your body, they told me. Believe in your ability to do this. Your body is designed to have children. Do not stiffen, they said, and do not be afraid. Open your arms, let it rush to meet you, try not to think of it as pain at all.

'Don't be frightened,' they said, but I didn't know how not to be, of this pain I was supposed to welcome in, a pain that my body held somewhere in its cells, readying itself to roar. However I looked at it, learned about the biology, the mechanics, I could not get beyond the idea that pain hurts.

Towards the end of my first pregnancy, tightening with a Braxton Hicks contraction, I would put a hand onto my stomach and think about the impending moment when my body and I would part company, brain versus flesh. You can be told over and over to embrace it, but that doesn't mean you will. It doesn't even mean you can.

When I was pregnant with my son, my second pregnancy, they tried to talk me back into a vaginal birth. 'It won't be as bad, this time around,' they said, and in those moments, sitting, smiling, my mind was frantic with animal fear, caught in the trap of my own body.

I pleaded, nicely, and I begged, politely, and I hated that doctor and the next, and the next, having to make my case over and over; and of course, most of all, I hated myself, even as I returned to the promise I had made, on the third day of my first labour: this will never happen again.

Then there's the episiotomy, which, in the run-up to childbearing, was something I thought about often. Too often? Certainly I worried more about it than I sensed was acceptable. 'Split ass to clit,' I remember overhearing in a bar, back in my twenties, and it was horrifying, but not unfamiliar; I knew from when I lost my virginity that anything to do with the area between my legs would result in pain before either productivity or satisfaction.

The NHS website was – is – prosaic. Other women, quiet. The internet, on the other hand, is ripe with discussion. It was with glutinous dread that I scrolled and read, about the stitching together of skin, and salt baths. What I couldn't find much on was the fear I was experiencing, fear shaded with outrage. The consent I had given was to have a baby; now I discovered that such consent encompassed, even instructed, a rampage across my most private parts.

Afterwards, my episiotomy stitched up without quite enough anaesthetic, unable to sit, to bend or lift, or move my bowels, I thought about reaching down to feel, but I was too afraid to touch, even to look. This, after all, is the stuff of nightmares.

Now, I wonder what I might have seen. When I do an internet search for the image I find that there are almost none of actual vulvas. There are many drawings, and some photos, of women with their hands crossed demurely across their pubic mound. A couple have covered their intimate hair with a question mark, or the letters 'SOS'. Too awful, then, for Google. No wonder I couldn't bring myself to see what had been done to me. Or, depending on how you look at it, what I had done to myself.

One study, cited in the *British Medical Journal*, concludes, 'Women receive little information in advance about episiotomy, yet the procedure has a wide range of physical and psychological consequences. This includes long-term anxiety about the damage done to them as women.' Here in the UK, the rate of episiotomies per birth is around 1 in 7, and around 90 per cent of women undergoing childbirth will tear.

In the face of all this, there is a temptation to assume that the rest of women's pain is comparatively trivial. The ineptly performed smear test, the shove of an IUD. The miscarriage; the pill-induced abortion. Even flushing a woman's fallopian tubes, a common procedure for those with difficulty conceiving, doesn't require an anaesthetic, apparently.

All this is pain repacked as 'discomfort'. 'You might feel some discomfort now,' they say, and 'might' generally means 'will'. And 'some'? 'Some' means, 'Don't complain, it's not forever, you're a woman and this is what women must endure.' Occasionally, it is followed by, 'At least it's better than being in labour, right?' – a quip which neatly sidesteps the fact we're not supposed to complain about that, either.

'You're not trying,' said the woman with her gloved hand in my vagina, on our third session of hard-won pelvic floor physiotherapy, many months later.

'I am,' I said, quietly, pleasantly; this woman was pen-
etrating me with her fingers, after all, and I did not want
to antagonise her. She was tall and willowy, her hair an
ashy blonde and a voice that suggested childhood skiing
trips, maybe a pony. If I had met her in a café or through
work we would not have been friends; of that, I had
no doubt. Yet here she was, inside me, her mouth tight
with disdain.

'It's not enough,' she said. 'You have to try harder.'

I wanted to say that I had tried.

I wanted to say that I was frightened my delivery had
damaged me in a way that could not be repaired. That
I had been left for hours with my baby jammed inside
me, while those who could have helped me were called
away over and over again to emergencies in theatre; that
I understood why this was so, but that since then, since,
finally, the doctor had cut me and pulled my daughter
out, I had felt broken, scarred, scared, and alone. That
for weeks, I had been afraid to shit lest I burst my rup-
tured perineum back open; that I'd sat though coffees,
lunches, a family tea party, smiled through the pain and
agreed when everyone told me how lucky I was. That I
had thought, hoped, prayed, that if I kept quiet, maybe
the pain would quieten, too.

I wanted to say that for the following eighteen months,
it had kept hurting. That inside me was different, in every
quantifiable sense *worse*. That it seemed to me I had spent
some vital currency in childbirth which I could not now
earn back.

That I had, finally, made an appointment with a doctor,
which took weeks to come round, and then I went and

listened to him dismiss everything I said. The despair, afterwards. The frantic internet searches, realising I was now that person, the woman who says, 'I know what's wrong with me,' her jaw set, even as she opens the consulting-room door. Another wait, another appointment. A referral, many more months of waiting, lost notes, complaints, half-hearted apologies.

And I wanted to say that, all this time, fighting the system, I was fighting myself, my urge to do nothing, to leave it, not to make a fuss. It was hard to get into a room to be seen, and it would be a different kind of hard, I knew, once I was inside.

I wanted to describe what it had taken, just to get me into that room: it had made me hate the system, hate my body; had, at times, made me hate my husband, who had become a parent without exertion, without physical pain. That my poor daughter had spent her first weeks with a mother who struggled to bond with her, who was angry, and resentful, and lonely, and frustrated, and sad.

I wanted to tell the cool, pale woman that I was ashamed I was even there, on the table, my legs apart, her gloved hand inside me, disappointing her, disappointing myself.

'I have been doing as much as I can,' I said.

'No,' she said. 'Everything is too weak.'

With that, she peeled off her glove and dropped it into the bin.

This may be why I am finding it so hard to tell you about my pain. If I can't be the woman who bleeds light and blue, then at least let me be the woman who is springy, eternally youthful and sweet with optimism. I know what she looks like and what she sounds like. I can do a fantastic impression of her; after all, she's who I used to be.

Where do I go from here? Back to silence, I suppose. I almost hit delete before this made it onto the page.

I know what is expected of me, and the last thing I want is to make anyone else feel uncomfortable. Which is why I suspect I'll end up just the same as before, colluding with the doctors and nurses, the women and the men. Back in the wordless state that renders women's pain invisible and irrelevant to anyone who is not going to be called into that warm room, asked to remove her trousers and cover herself with a paper towel.

Press It

'Press button?'

We are walking along the main road and my son is in the buggy and we pass a crossing and he sees it. His body stiffens and he rises from his seat, every atom of him straining towards his beloved.

'Want. Press it. Button.'

Never has anyone desired anything so wildly as my son, right now, gazing at the small black box by the pelican crossing.

Buttons in lifts and the button on the gate at nursery. The buttons at the Transport Museum, which is a kind of button fiesta. There are London buses – not even replicas of buses but actual London buses – cut in half, each containing a child thoughtfully spinning the steering wheel; a simulated Tube train cockpit, and, best of all, an entire replica street corner: traffic lights, green man, a button on each side, the lot. One rapturous afternoon, my son crossed and re-crossed the 'road' for an hour.

By comparison, my desires feel so mired in equivocation. I feel the press of them; I want *this* chair or *that* job.

But even as I do, I am thinking can I afford it, why do I want it, do I deserve it. What is the point of desiring anything, frankly, when the world is so uncertain.

When did I last plainly desire anything? When did I allow myself that pleasure?

To be a toddler, conversely, is to be in a state of near constant desire, and then, when the subject of that desire is almost inevitably withheld, to be overcome by rage. My job, I discover, is to somehow uproot the desire before it takes hold (*no, we do not play with the knife block*) or to imbue it with disgust (*absolutely no, you mustn't shake the abandoned can of Tennent's into your mouth*) or to thread it through with baffled resentment (again, the knife block), so that life becomes, instead, a series of frustrations internalised, pleasure limited and deferred. Which sounds pretty grim, and I suppose it is, but remains better than developing a drink problem at the age of two and a half.

I do still want things. What I seem to want most, these days, is to avoid disaster. *We can't be late, she mustn't be upset, will he be cold, and are there enough nappies?* The preparations for a picnic with friends take an hour, and once there, instead of relaxing, I stew in motherly fret. *Whose hands need cleaning and don't spill the juice and is anyone going to eat that chicken?* The children, meanwhile, are busy in the sandpit, or on the climbing frame, or, in my son's case, pulling up clumps of grass.

Because, oh, children, toddlers, they are so sharply alive. My daughter, tasting smoke in the air, my son running his fingers across the turf, and I see them noticing all of it, a world that was passing me by. Everything is a distraction because everything is fascinating – the texture of the sand, the distant dot of a helicopter, the weave of the blanket. I watch them and think, I want to go back to *this*, even as I am simultaneously thinking that there is someone I need to text back and should I apply for the teaching post and we need to buy milk.

'Want press button.'

We've got to drop that book back to the library and then go round Sainsbury's, and collect his sister from school, and rain is threatening and the box is set at a height he can't quite reach from his seat in the buggy and I could unclip him but then I'd have to get him back in and it would be easier just to go on and . . .

'Press it? Button?'

And, just this once, I stop, and gruntingly lift up the whole lot, so that his finger is level with that little white disc.

He doesn't press it straight away, but lets his finger hover over it for a second, two, three, savouring it, making sure that when he does, he will hit the exact centre, as my muscles scream and I mutter, *Come on, come on, come on.*

His finger goes out and – ah – his smile as the button goes in.

The light comes on, but we don't wait, we keep going, because we're late to the library, late to Sainsbury's, and, oh dear, running late now to get his sister, all because we stopped to push a button we didn't need to push, and stopped again ten metres down the road to push another, and then another, and another, and another.

We were late, so very late, and my God, it was worth it.

Bad Mother

Here are some of the things that have made me feel guilty over the course of the last twenty-four hours.

Chopping vegetables for my and my husband's dinner when I should have been playing with our two-year-old. It occurred to me that we could have explored the vegetables together, talked about their taste and texture. Instead, I told him to leave the kitchen.

Putting the television on when he asked for it, and allowing him to watch his favourite programme, of which he has seen every episode at least five times, instead of suggesting something new and potentially educational.

Hurrying my daughter when she wanted us to sit and look through her school books, because it was 8.20 p.m. and I wanted to eat. I did not hurry her much, not enough that she said anything, but I was aware that when she said, 'And here's my maths book from September,' I did reply, 'Not another one.' I regretted it then and I regret it now.

Ignoring my son for a couple of minutes when he was trying and failing to assemble a toy buggy until he yelled, 'Baby!' and burst into tears.

Feeding my children chicken nuggets for the fourth night in a row.

Letting them play at the dinner table while I served ice cream and not stepping in even when I vaguely suspected something untoward was going on. A moment later, my son, who had been standing on his chair, fell off onto the wooden floor. Now he has a yellow–purple bruise on his forehead the size of an egg.

Tuning out when they are speaking, because apparently my inner life is more interesting to me than the reality of my beloved children. 'What are you thinking about, Mummy?' my daughter asked last night. I was thinking about how much I needed to mop the floor.

Allowing myself to become irritated when they don't do what they are told straight away, even though I know full well that they're kids, not robots.

Talking to them while standing up, rather than bending down to engage with them at eye level as I know I should.

Looking at my phone when they are talking to me.

Looking at my phone instead of talking to them.

These are the events I can pin down, moments I can elucidate, and quantify. Then there is the ever-present, indescribable guilt that comes simply from being me, my fallible, ageing, selfish, corrupted, materialistic, dis-tracted, dissembling self.

Another one for the list, a list so long that it would pack out filing cabinets, whole rooms, even: leaving my son at nursery so that I could write this.

Bad mother. Bad mother. Bad mother.
How often do I say this to myself? Every week? Every

day? Every minute of every day? My life passes in a blaze of incessant internal chatter. So constant is the assailment that you would think I would no longer notice it. Maybe some people get used to feeling like this, but I never ever do.

'I'm a bad mother,' I say.

'*I'm* a bad mother,' say my friends, say my colleagues, say women I know and women I do not.

We say it when the snack is forgotten or the school shoes are too tight. A missed temperature, a lost toy, an after-work drink that turns into three and we say it: 'I'm such a bad mother.'

On we march, locked in step, faster and faster, loving and tending and feeding and nursing and snapping and barking and shouting and crying and beneath it all, *bad mother bad mother bad mother*, a drumbeat, a heartbeat, to which we live our lives.

There is a mother out there who does not feel guilty, because she does everything right.

Can you picture her? I can. A mash-up of the Virgin Mary, an M&S advert and the goddess Gaia, her face is tender and strong, and always – always – tilted down towards her child. This woman is everywhere; on billboards, in books and poems, rendered in film and song. She is wrapped in beauty, a mother's beauty, the gentle expression, modest clothing, soft to the touch. Her radiant and well-adjusted children are already rehearsing phrases like:

'Everything she did was for me.'

'A mother's love is like no other.'

'She sacrificed herself for us.'

I may only really have come face to face with her when I had a child of my own, but I have been raising her up ever since I understood what a mother is, what a mother should be.

If I wanted I could make a statue of her. Really, though, there's no need. She's already there, inside me, so tall that she blocks out the sun. There is no one more wonderful. And now that I am a mother myself, I see another truth: there is no one more ruthless.

I can feel her, watching me, eyes narrow, as I move from room to room, mumblingly inept, forgetting what I have come in for, remembering only when I am back downstairs.

She only has to raise a pristine eyebrow and I know that, once again, I am falling short. She is the backseat driver, the friend who inhales sharply as you reveal your new haircut, the expensively clad boss leaning over your desk as you type. She knows what to do, and I do not.

She polices my inner life, this mother. Every room is bugged, every thought monitored and found wanting. I defend myself, weakly, but I know that her judgement is correct.

Must try harder. Not good enough. Bad mother.

This smiling, unbending woman, she gives me strength – of a sort. Strength when there is none left, the flail as a whip smacks against raw skin. It is she who grips my shoulders, slaps my face. On you go.

In a way, I am grateful for her, my mumspiration, my yardstick, my governor in chief; without her, standards, already low, would slip into the gutter. And although I often want to send her packing, I am afraid that if I do, there will be no mother left. For, let's be honest, I am not doing my best all of the time. I am trying fairly hard, some of the time, and that is not the same thing.

But look. Glance through the camera roll on my phone, freeze-frame after freeze-frame of cheerful ease. Watch me at the playdate, at the birthday party, at your kitchen table. No shouting, no mindless scrolling. Listening and tending and caressing, performing verb after maternal verb. I display motherhood, a peacock's tail of Instagram posts, my happy children, sunny days.

See how good at this I – apparently – am.

In the week or so after a holiday, or lunch with friends, when I look back at the pictures I see only what is not there. The forgotten waterproofs and the playground trip abandoned after a fall into the mud. Unattended fingers trapped in a door. That fight over the crisps.

And then the reality fades, and I am left with a record of everything that worked. Only the good survives.

During the toughest times – the days after my children were born, those first weeks of lockdown – I did not take many photos, but those I did are full of love, of tenderness and joy.

These images sit entirely separately from my actual memories – not just on a different shelf but in a different place, another building. I don't want to visit it, much, and it certainly isn't open to the public. Let the dust thicken, the lock on the door grow stiff.

Instead, I linger in the gallery where the images of my best self are hung. See how we painted our faces and put all those clips in the baby's hair! Remember that morning when we made a cake! Look at the rainbow we painted and how we tacked it to the front window!

I do know how hard it was, I can still feel it, but I have bandaged the wound with these images as one might plaster up a blister, and got back on the road. 'It wasn't so hard, not in the end,' I say, to anyone who might be listening, I say to myself. Or, it was, but we got through it, and we even managed to have some fun along the way.

I know that these images are false, and that they are true. Perhaps it wouldn't matter, were it not that I believe in the good of others, and the bad of myself.

My friends are, on some essential level, kinder than me, more capable. Better mothers. I know this because I have sat in their kitchens and I have seen their photos. I scroll past other women, gathering up their laughing offspring, bestowing kisses, and think, yes! You are the one from the Book of Mummy, while I am just me, searching the NHS website with one hand and stirring burnt baked beans with the other.

I know this even as I upload the pictures of my own smiling family. For when it comes to propaganda, I am a compulsive consumer, and I generate it, too. As much as anyone.

'Do men feel like this?' wondered my friend, when I asked her whether she felt a tenth as bad as me.

'I don't know,' I said. And I don't.

I do know that the bar is lower for men. Unlike those of us who become pregnant and give birth, they are able to maintain for longer the façade that their lives are, in both essence and practical terms, unchanged. (Some men maintain it forever. Maybe they even believe it.)

Even for dedicated fathers, it's just *different*. Men are applauded more, and for much less. I recall my husband holding our seven-month-old, while I nipped into a hotel function room to watch my cousin getting married. 'What a great dad,' said a starry-eyed hotel employee, which meant that I spent the wedding pissed off that my husband had garnered praise for simply holding his own baby.

'It's my day with them and I just do this and it's bloody impossible,' said a dad friend once, as we sat with his little girls in a café. 'But when it's Clare's turn I know she'll do a proper lunch and housework and make our dinner. But.' And here he shrugged. *What can you do?*

I know that there are advantages for men, living alongside eternally guilt-ridden women. For someone else to have hoisted the needs of the household onto her back; to keep the bathroom clean and the fridge stocked with cucumber and broccoli that no one much fancies.

Not all men and not every man all the time, and forgive me – bad mother, bad writer – for generalising. But.

Eye tests and nicely wrapped birthday presents and not that brand of sippy cup but this one, and should we get a paddling pool before the heatwave next week and the sunblock is out of date and the kids' feet need measuring and while we're there: welly boots.

To put down the whip. To lower the bar.

It sounds simple and it feels impossible, and somewhere between the two is where I am, oscillating between I should and I can't, I want and I won't. For as long as the society I inhabit continues to venerate the perfect mother, I will despise the parts of myself that exist outside of her demands.

Sometimes I wonder why it is that I can see so clearly the impossibility of all this, the stupidity of it, yet still be unable to free myself. However hard I – we – try, it will never be enough; not while the mothers in our collective mind's eye inhabit this higher plane, outside the realm of fallible humanity. Why is it that I am still servile to this sexism, the destruction it wreaks upon me, and, in turn, upon those I love?

It is because I am my children's mother, the noun and the verb. When I am ill, when I am exhausted, when I am awake, and when I am asleep. From now until I die, and every breath in-between, I am their mother, always.

And here I am.

Human. Checking my phone. Going out instead of reading a bedtime story. Knowingly, deliberately, giving my children chicken nuggets four nights in a row, because it's easy, because I'm tired, just because.

My daughter looks at her plate, and then back to me, and I shrug and say, 'You'll cope,' and it feels like a radical act.

And then the chicken nuggets are eaten, and everyone is back in front of the telly, and the beat goes on, *bad mother, bad mother, bad mother*, but just a little quieter, now.

Part 5

Month by Month, Moment to Moment

The Most Important Job

When I was eight months pregnant with my daughter, my skin developed a strange mark, strange enough for my GP to send me to hospital.

'I can just burn that off,' said the doctor whose office I was filling. 'Normally, you'd have to come back. But since you're . . .' He gestured at my stomach.

He was extremely alpha, this doctor; the sort who sits on the Tube with legs splayed at ninety degrees. He wanted me to know that he was doing me a favour and that I should be grateful. Which I was. Not quite as grateful as he'd have liked, perhaps, but grateful nonetheless.

As he readied the equipment, he chatted away at me about this and that, while I sat, meek and waiting.

'What is it that you do?' he asked, eventually.

'I'm a writer.'

The consultant's face changed, and then he began to laugh. I could tell that I had, in some sense, capitulated; he had me where he wanted me.

'You won't get much writing done, when you have a baby.'

Then, delighted with himself, he laughed some more.

★

For as long as I can remember, I have been making homes.

Houses for my dolls when I was six; fairy lights around the mirror at fourteen; the neat room with its fresh flowers in my student halls. In my early twenties, even when I was too poor to buy a travel card, I would still bake cakes, when I could, and change my sheets once a week. How I loved an orderly desk, a clean carpet, lighting a scented candle.

And even more, I loved the expression of delight on a man's face when I presented him with a pile of neatly folded clothes. Once, I went over to a boyfriend's house and found he had not done the washing for several weeks and had nothing to wear. I washed it all, every garment. *Look what I did! See what a good woman I am.* I recall, too, how quickly the delight faded and in its place came expectation: someone will ring the landlord, fix that toilet seat, look after me when I'm sick, fill the fridge.

'I just like to see things clean and tidy,' a new mother friend said, recently. I think, often, about where it comes from, this compulsion she has, we both have, to make things nice. Baking and washing and cleaning, no one made me do these things. It's not the same as it was for my grandmother, for her grandmother, for all the women, creating homes for their children, looking at their daughters and hoping that for the next generation, maybe life would hold something more than preparing food and mopping the floor. They were my choices. At least, I thought they were. The dinners I cooked, the floors I hoovered for all those men, the boyfriends and the flatmates; how well I looked after them, a living re-enactment of all the picture books and adverts, the bustling women in the homes of my family and friends, who in turn were following their mothers, and theirs, and theirs.

What I want to say is that these busy homemakers were revered by those around them (children, men) and beloved for their work. But I do not think this was the case, not for a moment. They did as they were expected, but if anyone appreciated them (and perhaps, to do so fully, one must have a sense of the kind of toil and toll it took) it was other women. When I trotted into the kitchen at the family party, aged all of nine years old, ready to hand out plates of cake, it was because I had become aware of what it is to be a nice girl, a girl who is helpful; a girl who is good.

It is a tricky business, these days, being a woman. We can do anything, *should* do anything; that's what we're told. Get out there, into the great wide world. It's just that we also have to do everything else, and by that, I mean, all the things that women have always done.

What of men? Is there any awareness that they have to engage with all of this? Not just be around and not just to help. Not to take orders and tick things off lists, but *to make the lists in the first place*. If there has been a corresponding message that men, too, must make their homes in order for women to live the lives we have been promised, it has been delivered in little more than a whisper, and consistently – and conveniently – goes unheard.

Looking back on my youth, my stomach turns. All the energy that I put into being sweet and pleasant, that I put into making myself a springboard from which others could launch – I could have used it in raising my voice. Hustling for work, making money, getting in the room. I could have been going out dancing or getting onto a train across the Himalayas. Instead of helping others, others who didn't care whether I helped them or not, I could – and, dammit, should – have been helping and pleasing myself.

Now I share my home with three people, two of whom genuinely can't cook or clean (unlike the men of my twenties, whose bemusement on such topics enrages me still). And so my husband and I must do this over and over and over, and the pleasure I once took in it has turned sour.

Perhaps I shouldn't be surprised. Instead of demonstrating my suitability for a role, trying it on for an afternoon (and, let's face it, indulging in a bit of cute role play) I no longer have any choice in the matter. It was my decision to make a home, yes. I did not know that homes must be remade daily, sometimes hourly.

I wish that my younger self had stayed out of the kitchen. I stand at the sink and I wish with all my might that she had gone back to the party, and danced.

It's not that I didn't experience sexism before I became a parent. I have been patted on the head and on the bum, told to 'get yourself a man'. I am small, and blonde, and polite, and in the eyes of many I have encountered over the years, such qualities simply cannot coexist alongside intelligence and ambition. 'Woman have now achieved equality,' a boyfriend once told me, and even then I knew there was a lot wrong with this statement; not least, that it was being delivered as inarguable fact by a twenty-something man fresh out of university.

Still, I never felt backed into a corner in the way that I do now. The minute-by-minute battles that I must wage, along with the constant and painful unpicking of what my husband and I thought we knew and thought we shared.

If anyone had suggested including 'obey' in our wedding vows, we would have laughed them out of the room. 'Of course I won't submit to my husband, and nor would he want me to,' I – and he – would have said. Fast forward a few years, though, and I can't even nip out for milk until he gets home. Who steps in when the child is sick, on the inset days; who is around when the precious weeks of annual leave fall wildly short of the school holidays? Mine is the number that automatically gets the call from school, mine is the career that withers as my energy is poured into the family. But these are *our* children, *our* home.

It could be split, 50:50, but it's not, because logic suggests – and by suggests, I mean dictates – that it should be the part-timer, the lower earner, the flexible one; and that means me, the mother, just as it does in almost every other partnership I know.

We could swap, I suppose. He could stay home and I could take up the mantle of (that awful word) 'breadwinner'. My salary took a hit during my two periods of maternity leave, so we would be materially poorer, and that's before we even get to the various gender assumptions, both external and entrenched, over who does what. And suddenly it's feminism versus the granite of reality, and I'd always assumed that they were the same thing. But no. Or at least, not yet.

What I want is to be in a position for us both to parent and to earn. And here's the nub: I thought that this was the world in which we already lived. Or, if not, then I thought we could make it so. That *I* could make it so, by sheer force of being right.

I thought this right up until I was wheeled onto the postnatal ward.

Now, when I get the text, or see the Facebook update, or the friend leans in and squeezes my arm and whispers, 'I'm pregnant,' I'm delighted for her. I'm sorry, too, for what she is about to discover.

I think of us, the women, educated and empowered and excited for what comes next, fresh meat to be ground through the ancient problem. We're feminists and if we're lucky we are sharing our lives with feminists. It's not actually about who does the dishes and changes the nappies, is it? We don't even need to say this to one another, it's so bloody obvious.

Then baby comes and the front door swings shut and suddenly it's 1954.

'What do you do?' people ask, but what they mean is, 'Who are you?' and in my answer, there it was, my understanding of myself.

Before I had a child, I wrote and I taught. I taught some days and I wrote most days, with varying levels of success, both in terms of my bank balance and in the quality of what was on the page. I am extraordinarily lucky, in that my job is the thing I most want to be doing; putting words on the page, the right words, in the correct order, is the best way I can think of to spend my time. But even when this has not been so, my work has, at the very least, been how I have spent my day. And this is no small thing.

Work is what I – we – do. Work is understood. It is respected. Work is important.

Important, that is, until I had children, and then, while it was no less important, somehow everything else became *more* important. And for the first time in my adult life, I was asking myself, why is it that I work at all?

Here is something no one told me, or that just wasn't interesting enough for me to truly take on board before I had a baby: every pound of what I would earn until they went to school would be spent on childcare. Every last pound. Sometimes, often, quite a lot more.

'It's our money,' my husband said, and I agreed; what he earned was ours and what I earned was ours. Still, after a year's maternity leave, returning to work part-time meant that it was impossible for me not to equate the money I earned with the money that we were spending on childcare. Especially when they amounted to the same thing.

I find it *creepy*, not being able to earn enough of my own money. Or, more accurately, being able to earn money in theory but not in practice, because even to attempt to earn more money requires more childcare, and more childcare costs more money, money that we do not have.

When I think about money, I recall my pregnancy. My pregnancy with our child. Now, it is my husband's task to earn our money, and just as, in the end, my husband could not complete his ownership of the pregnancy or of the experience of tending a newborn, so I could not, still cannot, seem to take full ownership of the money he has earned. We talked about this, agreed that we are a team and that in looking after our children I am earning our money too. Yet without the figures on the screen at the end of the month, a large part of me refuses to believe it.

If I am tempted by, say, a nice sandwich, my mind buzzes with words like 'frippery' and 'indulgence', although I know full well it would be a sandwich my husband would buy himself, and that he would encourage me to have it, were he by my side.

I don't need his permission, I say to myself, as I hesitate over a book, or a jumper; over anything not directly connected to the household, remembering the old jokes about wives and their shopping habits.

At home, with no boss, no way to gauge how well I am doing and no fixed hours, every action becomes fraught with self-recrimination. I – we – try to equate the labour of motherhood with that of employment; it cannot be done. This is a simplicity that I miss from my old life, the exchange of a chunk of my time and effort for numbers on a bank statement.

When work does not mean money, when, in my case, and surely so many others, it in fact meant debt, when it left me stressed and tired and anxious, torn between my home and my desk, one might legitimately ask the question: why are you doing this? No one did, but it was something I constantly asked myself.

It is hard for me to admit that I am working because I want to. For we are caught in a paradox. All our lives we have been told that work is essential, and, simultaneously, that there is no more important job than being a mother.

Now my work had become why we had so much less money than before, and the shame of it hung in a cloud around me even as I said (trying not to look at the bill, no, I won't have a coffee, thanks, and do we really need to fix the roof this year?) 'I am working now so that I have a job in five years' time,' and, 'I am working because I want to set an example to my children.' Because work had become crazy, an aberration, something that needed to be justified.

My children have accepted that Daddy has a job to do and leave him to it. Despite lots of talk about how Mummy must do her work too, when I head out or sit down at my desk, it's clear that as far as they are concerned, my job is to be with them. I should probably consider where this has come from. Maternity leave? The skirted figures pushing shopping trollies, the picture books, the ratio of male to female faces at the school gate? Is this, too, somehow my fault?

Why am I even bothering, I ask myself, unlocking my computer for a twenty-minute stint that I know will be cut short. Why not give in to the inevitable and let them have me? Everything is suffering from this attempt to remove myself, even fleetingly, from the home: the children, my husband, my husband's work, my work. Me.

'How do you relax?' ask the surveys, and I think, *with work, of course.* (That the most relaxed part of my day is spent doing the opposite of relaxation tells me that I need to do something about all this, but God knows when I'll ever find the time to address it.) Work is my escape hatch, a way to find and reclaim myself.

Mind you, for me and for many of the mothers I know, the room of one's own is often measured in notion rather than square feet. Mothers working at the kitchen table, clearing space between the dinner plates and homework diaries. Answering emails for twenty-five minutes in a leisure centre carpark. Mothers taking calls on the bus, jotting guilty notes on their phones in the playground to loud cries of 'MUMMY, PUSH ME!'

The women who rise at 4 a.m. to work for two hours while the rest of the household sleeps, my God, those women.

'I find that I work better since I had kids, that I'm more focused,' said a friend with two children, going on to tell me how she wrote an entire presentation in the precious child-free hour on the train between Cambridge and Kings Cross.

When I sit down to work, assailed from all sides, managing to spit out maybe fifty words here, a hundred there, I think that they are all the better for being so hard won. Cereal bowls and unopened post, the shopping list and the washing pile – these are, in fact, exactly what I need.

It's only every now and then that I stop and think, really? Few are the acts of concentration that gain from too little time and constant distraction. No one wants surgery or even their car repaired in thirty-second bursts by someone who is simultaneously frying sausages and fielding messages on the class WhatsApp.

Perhaps we do work better and harder for having had our children. But if I were structuring my ideal working day, it would not be four hours long with seven unexpected breaks and on a night of no sleep. In fact, I don't know a single woman who would work in this way, given any kind of choice.

It's fucking hard, and if I tell people, their solution – give it up! – is obvious, and that's fucking hard too, just differently hard, and my desires have backed me into a corner, stupid woman, modern woman, wanting so much. It's not like this is a new conversation, and yet seven years on from my first birth I remain, to a greater or lesser extent, in shock, that this has happened, in London, in 2021, to me.

Sometimes I think how excellent I would be at being a man. A divide between professional life and home life that, if not quite clean, is certainly not the messy cat's cradle of womanhood. To work free of my motherhood, a person among other people, for it to be assumed that I am just and entirely myself, that's the goal, isn't it?

If I am tempted, indeed keen, to unmother myself, it is at least in part because, in the world of work, motherhood is so frantically undesirable. The taint of it, its trail of Sudocrem and odd socks. An enemy to the free-floating intellect, and besides, so unprofessional. To put on the clean clothes and click-clack my way onto the train feels like raising myself up, pushing away the lunch boxes and the grasping hands, ascending to some higher plain. I want my work to be received like that of a man, and that means working like a man, doesn't it?

So I say nothing about my other life. I turn in the piece at midnight and hope no one notices the time stamp. Reply to the urgent email, trying not to mention that I can't get back to my desk after school pick-up, trying not to mention the children at all, come to that. Skim over my fissures with hard work, harder than ever, and an easy smile.

I have everything I wanted – a family, an interesting job – but more often than not, the weight of my life leaves me on my knees. If the fulfilment of my desires is crushing me then the fault is internal; it has to be, doesn't it?

Family is good. Work is good. Which leads to the inevitable conclusion that it is me who is not.

To state the alternative out loud – that it is partners, employers, co-workers, the government, that are no good – feels incendiary, dangerous, even. It's all dangerous, which is why I suspect it has for so long been reframed by our society as tedious. There is no better way to remove threat.

Because it is a threat to the established order of things, to say that it's not that women should mother less, it's that fathers should father more. And it's not that parents are the enemy of the world of work, it's that all of us – the parents, the sisters, the brothers, the children, those with fragile parents, with friends in need, the carers, and those caring for their tender, wounded selves – we're all bound up together, and the less energy we expend on concealing our home lives from those with whom we work, the more we will have to get it all done.

These words are not threatening, because there is very little sense that anyone is listening, still less that times will change. I'm not surprised that I never noticed how angry and how broken mothers are, because unless you're a mother yourself, who cares?

Something is saying to me, as strongly as it knows how, that none of this is of interest to anyone. It is the moaning of a middle-class white woman who has no idea how good she's got it. It is hardly worth even acknowledging, and certainly not worth any scrutiny.

If I had to put a face to this something, it would be the face of that laughing consultant.

Is it my victory, or my foolishness, that I am still here? At the hob and at my desk, building myself, building my family, trying to make something more from all that I am lucky enough to have. Generations of women, toiling to make it better, not for themselves, but for their daughters. Women standing on each other's shoulders, raising each generation as high as they can, saying, 'I want you to have everything I could not.'

I want all this for my daughter, I want it for the women who came before me, and I want it for me. This is what I never foresaw, when I was young – that merely stating my life now is important would seem as if it were a direct contradiction to my womanhood. How selfish, how revolutionary it would feel, to say that I want as much from my time as I can. To demand a life of love and of work, of heart and mind.

This is what I would say to that man, if I could see him now.

I will make it happen. I will get it done. It will not be perfect, not by any means. Motherhood may have ignited my rage, sharpened my hunger and focused my love, but there are days when I lie broken upon its wheel.

There will be other days.

For this, too, I have discovered: I have the fruits of the labours of all those women who came before me. As my children grow older and more independent, I even have a little time.

My job, now, is to live the rest of my life, all of my life. To live it well.

And on some days, and in the right light, I think it – and I – could be strong, and beautiful, and good.

Zoom Zoom Zoom

We knew from the second they started coming down the wooden steps. Clutching them. Or towing them. Or, in the most extreme cases, inside them, peering out.

'We've been junk modelling!' says the classroom assistant.

Junk modelling, aka making things out of rubbish. Or, as another parent memorably put it, 'Sticking bits of crap to other bits of crap.'

The dad next to me gets off fairly lightly, with a contraption made of yogurt pots. If he wasn't immediately aware of his good fortune, he comes to see it in full as the next child steers herself down the steps, shouting, 'Beep, beep! I've made a CAR.'

'You *have*,' says her mum. 'And isn't it . . . big.'

Cardboard, some the rough-hewn brown of loo rolls and Amazon packages, some from cereal boxes and flyers with the technicolour shine of tropical beetles. The frosted plastic of milk bottles. Parcel tape and Sellotape, already unfurling, so that the clutched objects drag long and sticky tentacles, a shoal of steam-punked jellyfish.

In her hands, my daughter holds what she tells me is a

rocket. 'To go to the moon with.' She is so proud, and, walking home beside her as she bears it in her arms, I am proud too. I can picture the afternoon of work that went into it, the careful arrangement, a slip of tongue poking between her teeth.

'It's like the song,' I say. '"Zoom Zoom Zoom". Do you remember?'

She shakes her head.

'I sang it to you when you were a baby,' I tell her.

> Zoom zoom zoom
> We're going to the moon
> Zoom zoom zoom
> We'll be there very soon
> Five
> Four
> Three
> Two
> One
> BLAST OFF!

'Oh right,' she says, not much interested.

So I try bringing it back to the present, saying, 'And now my baby has made a rocket all of her own!'

Five steps later, said rocket is already threatening to fall apart. We put it in her bedroom, in the corner. Bin day is in less than a week. I just hope she doesn't notice.

Forget the suits who spend their lives in business class, the four-by-fours and single-use plastic; the absolute worst thing you can do to the environment is have children.

The stats are easy enough to come by, but I don't even

need to be told, emptying the party bag or squishing yet another soiled nappy into the refuse sack before sending it off to landfill. Some days, I look out at the bobbing sea of toys that is our sitting-room floor, think of the Pacific garbage patch, and feel faint.

The wrappers. Twists of burst water balloons. The wipes, oh, the wipes! What's wrong with kitchen roll and water? Or a good old-fashioned damp cloth? Nothing, except the smell, and the wriggling horror that would show up under a microscope, and the admin of all those hot washes and . . . So, wipes it is, and I've just googled and each individual wipe will be with us for (dear God) one hundred years.

That uneaten fish finger, limp with ketchup, on the edge of the plate. I think of the fish that swam, that were hauled up on a boat, gills groaning for water as their tails hit the white walls of their polystyrene tombs. The fields of whatever it is that makes the crumb – corn? Wheat? The supermarket, the hum of the freezer, the journey to our kitchen. 'You really don't want it?' I say, mindful that in this house, We Do Not Waste Food, before popping it into a Tupperware box, where it sits in the fridge for days. Outside it is 6°C. Inside, the house has been gas heated and insulated and holds steady at 19°C, and inside *that* is the fridge, a symphony of rubber, plastic, enamel and aluminium, which has been cooled back down to 6°C and if I think about all this for more than twenty seconds I will be sick, sending yet more food down the drain.

My family, my beautiful family, four of the eight billion, two of whom were added despite the sure knowledge that the world is groaning with our kind, that we are pulling it apart. When I see people in great numbers, at festivals or in a stadium, I am reminded of swarming cockroaches. Then I take my children into my arms and think of the mother roach, who probably adores her babies, too.

We rush, we push, we take, we colonise. We probably *are* going to the moon, and Mars, at some point, partly for the sheer joy of it, and partly because we're trashing our own planet so comprehensively that, like those couples on *Location, Location, Location* who would prefer to re-mortgage than declutter, it seems easier to simply move on.

There's even rubbish in space, these days. Right now, NASA is actively tracking more than 27,000 pieces of what it calls 'orbital debris'. Whether we're going to the moon or not, our crap has already landed.

Seen written for the first time, my defence is so flimsy it does not seem worth the paper it will be printed upon.

We buy local and use up leftovers. Toys are second-hand. Most of the kids' clothes are hand-me-downs, from charity shops and car boot sales and eBay. We're doing our best, right?

Come on, though. That's not the whole story or anything like it. We take public transport but keep a car. Most of our clothes are second-hand, but some – the pants and socks and T-shirts – are from Primark and H&M. 'Fast fashion . . .' says a friend, dubiously, and she's right. A Primark T-shirt will last two summers, one for us and one for someone else's child, but probably not the one after, or the one after that; yet I balk at spending ten times the cost to keep it from landfill one day, in the future, at a time out of my control.

Even second-hand doesn't really help. My son's favourite garment, the perfect fleece, snuggly and stain-proof, is
made of polyester and sheds zillions of its fibres in each
wash, fibres that will surely lodge in the brains of unborn
foetuses and linger in the polar ice caps, at least until they
melt, which I suppose means they won't have to wait
around too long.

Toys are never new, unless it's a birthday or Christmas
and the grandparents say, 'What would they like best?'
and I send the inevitable link to Argos. (Also, toys outside
birthday and Christmas, what luxury! What unnecessary
luxury.) We could be vegetarian. We are, emphatically,
not.

And we consume. We consume and consume and
consume. Not just food, although Christ, we get through
food, the quantities somehow much greater than simply
four times what I bought when it was only me. The tissues and the bleach and the washing machine chuntering,
always, while the dishwasher gargles chemicals and hot
water just a couple of metres away.

We power through stuff, mouths and arms wide open,
like Pac-Man; like Jaws. And by having kids I've both
made the problem worse, and I have made it theirs.

And what do I do about it? Not enough. Because
nothing is really enough; short of going off grid in an
eco-lodge, nothing will ever be enough – and even that
probably isn't enough. Which is not an excuse for not
doing it, I don't have an excuse for not doing that, but I
am not doing that. I'm doing the other thing, the shameful thing. I'm hoping it will, somehow, all go away.

★

'There is junk at the bottom of the ocean,' says my daughter, on the way home from school one afternoon. Her shock is huge and terrible. 'There are people who put rubbish in the sea and it is polluting the planet. Even a whale died.' She looks up at me, boggling. 'A WHALE, Mummy.'

Oh darling, I think, as I say, carefully, 'Yes. I have heard about that.'

Her step quickens, her hand grips mine: this is urgent. 'We've got to do something.'

'Yes.' I think hard. 'What would you like to do?'

What she would like to do, it transpires, is to save the whole world. I don't know how to point out that this is incompatible with the entirety of life as she currently knows it. Instead, I mumble something about making sure we only buy things that we really need. And eating all the dinner on our plates (then the spectre of an eating disorder looms and I rephrase this, clumsily, into only eating until we are full and then saving the rest for later). And being careful with things like putting the lids back on felt-tips and not wasting paper.

'Should I not do drawing, then?' asks my daughter, forlorn.

'Of course you can do drawing,' I say, while thinking, probably not, no. We probably shouldn't do *anything*, but having put her here, I can't just make her life shit to atone for humanity's sordid past, and besides, a few sheets of A4 are probably not the difference between rainforest and dustbowl.

'It's not a crime to be human,' says a friend. It's not, but also, it is.

We go for a day out in Brighton. My daughter beetles off in an attempt to pick up every piece of litter on the beach. We follow, at a distance, ready to lunge between her and broken glass.

Later, in bed, she says it again. 'I just really want to save the world.'

It's shaming, to be faced with such resolve. I, too, want to save the world. I think. Maybe. What I actually want is for the world to be saved by someone else, so that I can stop worrying about it.

Unlike my daughter, as an adult, indeed a middle-class Western adult, I am in a position of particular privilege when it comes to world-saving. Yet my tiny acts of virtue feel like a pipetted drop into the polluted ocean. I diligently pass the importance of recycling, using public transport and the like onto the rest of the household, only privately speculating as to the point. It won't save us, not even close. But my children have to believe it will; the alternative is too terrifying.

As a child of the Eighties, of CFCs and the hole in the ozone layer, I am aware that my determined non-engagement with any of this is a luxury my kids will not have. There is something of a rabbit-in-headlights freeze to my inertia, which is awful. And then there is the sense that in any oncoming collision, my children are the shield. Which is much, much worse.

I could give it to them straight. Keep the TV running through the bit where David Attenborough explains how comprehensively fucked everything is. Read it, everything, read it all. I don't, because I want to protect them, despite being aware that 'protect' in this particular context is eccentric at best.

It's shameful, and cowardly, and it's perverse. Their fear, their rage; both would give them a better chance when it's their turn to fix things, and yet I don't want my children weeping their nights away in terror. I want them comfortable, in their cosy beds, in their centrally heated house, and yes, I know that this is wrong. But I do not know how to balance my need for everything to be OK with the reality, which is that there is plenty to worry about, and it is not.

My children. I don't want you to find out that we ruined it all for you, that your very existence is making it worse. The world should be a golden gift, and you believe that it is, and I can't bear to tell you the truth, not yet.

Perhaps I could, if I knew of a way to feel empowered, but it all feels too enormous, too far beyond my control. And too sad.

There's too much stuff, these days. There always has been, but it is worse now. The unboxing craze which spawned that pinnacle of wastefulness, the LOL Surprise!, its surprise being a massive plastic ball filled with twiddly bits of plastic crap, each wrapped in yet more plastic, oh God oh God. The other marketing craze, for the opposite, the unbleached cotton and the blond wood, beeswax and hemp, which I bought into, for a while, before realising that the opposite of buying something is to buy nothing.

The kids love it. They love it all. Every advert is a new opportunity for desire. 'Can I have this? And that? And this?'

It's illuminating, to see consumerism without the trappings and coatings with which we conceal it to ourselves. When I fancy buying something, I make excuses. 'Oh, I do actually need a top with sleeves this length.' Or, 'These shoes will be so useful.' Watching my children walk past the shops, I think, no, this is what I am truly feeling. The terrible, planet-destroying lust for new things. All that lovely, gorgeous, dizzyingly delightful *stuff*.

The shiny sequins that you can rub up and down to reveal a hidden picture, and on a T-shirt! Glittery beach shoes, dinosaur eggs that take three tantalising days to 'hatch'. Fidget spinners and bubble wrappers – and they want it all and I want to give it to them and I don't, mostly. But I can't bring myself to entirely despise it, either.

That is, until I see it all piled up on the floor.

'Everything is plastic,' said my daughter, sadly. We'd gone to a toy shop to choose birthday presents. It should have been a moment of triumph, but in fact, I hated watching her wrestle back her excitement, wanting everything, trying not to.

'You can still have birthday presents,' I said. 'Just make sure you play with them, lots. And when you're finished with them, we'll give them to someone else.' Virtuous, yes. Hardly wild and untrammelled joy.

The next day, collecting my two-year-old son from nursery, the room leader took me to one side. 'We've been doing recycling,' she said. 'Please could you reinforce the difference between cardboard and glass?'

'Yes,' I said, with sudden, useless, resolve. 'We can and we will.'

Zoom zoom zoom
We're going to the moon

'Blast off!' shouts my little boy, finding his sister's junk-modelled rocket, running into the garden and waving it at the greying London sky. It has already shed its nose cone and now the toilet-paper contrail breaks free, falls onto the plastic grass.

Will they hate me? Or will they be grateful that I gave them just a few years of innocence, maybe the final few that any of us will have, before it all comes crashing down?

Zoom zoom zoom
We'll be there very soon

The Land of Make-Believe

'The tooth fairy has a purple hat,' said my daughter's friend Lucie. 'And a cloak, with stars on it. She can fly. But she doesn't come down the chimney.'

'Because that's how Father Christmas comes in?'

'Because she would get messy,' said Lucie, in a tone that made clear she was talking to an idiot. 'She comes in through the window. You've forgotten because you are big.' Then, deciding that she had delivered as much information as her intellectually challenged audience could absorb in a single sitting, she went back to her episode of *Hey Duggee*.

I haven't forgotten. While she was talking, my tongue was back exploring the new space in my mouth, a caldera of gum, the slow and fascinating rise of new adult teeth. The wonder of waking up and finding a coin under my pillow, the particular smell of the metal, hot from my clutch, the weight of it in my palm. I remember it again a few nights later, pushing the door to my daughter's bedroom and wincing with each footstep and creak. Every visit from the tooth fairy, each Christmas morning, we hold the thrill of our child selves with the power of our adulthood and it's like being given a magic wand that works every time.

Let's not over-egg this: when you're small, it's hard to find something that *isn't* miraculous. A tap of the debit card and the forbidden muffin is ours. Humans can't levitate, but see, there's a helicopter. And a fairy comes in the middle of the night to exchange coins for human teeth.

My children believe in the tooth fairy. They believe in Father Christmas. And when they look at me, they see the marvellous . . . the miraculous . . . Mummy!

I made a child, with sex and food and time, and then I did it again. I have taught the speechless to talk, manoeuvred wees beyond counting into the potty. Dispenser of the Calpol, creator of cheesy pasta; nightmares flee at my embrace. I measure out our lives in booster jabs and Savlon, swimming nappies and the Gruffalo. None shall touch the KitKat tin, except Me.

'I'm scared,' says my daughter, on the morning of a new term, a whole new school year.

'It'll be OK,' I tell her, shivering in my arms.

'How do you know?'

'I just do,' I say.

She has to believe me.

And she does.

'You know that I wasn't always a mummy,' I say one day, and explain that I once had another life, so recently that I still have its books, clothes, mugs, its stock cubes, probably. She nods; yes, she knows, but I can see from the blankness of her gaze that she doesn't feel it. And I discover that I am speaking in a language she cannot yet understand.

During her twenties, my mum lived in London, a flat in a crumbling Crouch End mansion, and every time we drove past it, she would tell us of the cold, her housemates, the mushrooms that grew beside the bath.

We would listen, but it didn't feel real, even as she described it, even as the house itself rushed by. Everything before me is before time, because although my mum was, I was not. Sometimes, I feel the pull of that mist, and sense my own memories, my pre-motherhood existence, slipping into the shadowlands, and I understand all that talk of flatmates and fungi, because it's then that I reach for the photos, text old friends, message my little sister, trying to reassure myself that even without my children bearing witness, I was, nonetheless, alive.

'But where is Boots now?' asks my daughter, when I come home with the empty cat carrier. We talk about memories, stars in the sky, the connectedness of everything. 'There's a book that will help,' says a friend, and I steel myself for a chat about the Bible. Thank the Lord, it's *Goodbye Mog*.

What is war and why isn't there YouTube in the car? Who is that man sitting outside Asda, asking for money, and what do you mean some people don't have homes and why can't he live in ours? How do people get chicken pox and why are we hurting the planet?

I don't know because I'm not God, I want to say, and also, I don't even know if even I believe there *is* a God, but before the words are formed, my children are in a screaming tangle on the rug.

The patience He must have! I regard my daughter, covered in chocolate milkshake, and wonder, how did she ever think that she could drink that *and* leapfrog over the sofa? Poor exhausted God, looking down into the Garden of Eden and saying, 'I told you not to eat it.' And while I aspire to understanding and forgiveness, on the days when there simply aren't enough cheeks to turn, it's the Old Testament I end up channelling, my fire and brimstone raining down from the top of the stairs.

It wasn't supposed to be like this. Before I had children, I had a decent idea of the kind of mother I would become. I had done my research, i.e. seen women bickering with their children in post office queues, and I'd read a few novels in which mothers orbited the main characters, occasionally entering the main plot for just long enough to damage them beyond repair. From this, a bit of watching friends who were already parents, and from grievances tenderly nursed through my own childhood, I came up with a character I could inhabit with any children I might produce.

The mother I planned to be did shout, but not properly and hardly ever. She took a keen interest in her children's development while holding back enough to give them freedom to create and be themselves. She was patient, appropriately firm, had an infinite supply of cuddles. And she smelled gorgeous.

Of course, this wouldn't be the whole me, I reasoned. She would be someone I would put on when needed; someone who, at the end of the day, I could shuck and regain my true self. 'Mummy' would be something to step into as necessary, like Clark Kent putting on his glasses. Shrug on a cardigan, grab a bunch of tulips, and look out, kids, here she comes!

Sometimes, the enchantment holds. I know that in forty-five seconds the banged elbow will stop hurting. Those cool hands, pressed to foreheads, applying plasters and tying shoes, they are now mine. This is the motherhood I want, and it's what I see, in the adverts and standing outside nursery, at friends' houses and in pictures on my phone: motherhood, pretty and plush.

Mostly, though, 'The Marvellous Mummy Show' is music, it is lights, and it is praying that no one slips backstage to find the wig and the vodka. It's that old dream of finding yourself on stage without a script, only all day, every day, and for real. When I glance in the mirror (which, like everything else here, needs cleaning) I see only myself. *Help me*, I mouth at my reflection. I don't know what I'm doing. Please. Someone? Anyone?

'Oh, it was awful,' said my own mother, when, finally, after whole years had elapsed, I managed to whisper my ineptitude. 'I didn't have a clue. And when you screamed . . .' I tell her I'm sorry, but she's hardly listening, transported back to 1979. 'And we didn't have the internet or mobile phones then. You have so many more resources now. We just had to get on with it.'

So many more resources! The Facebook groups and the Mumsnet threads, the books that can be conjured up in a single click. Whole empires have been built upon our collective uncertainty. All of human knowledge crowding onto a screen, everything I need is there, ready and waiting, if I just had the time to read it, the wit to parse it, the rigour to sift though it . . . and, oh look, I'm back exactly where I started.

Maybe that's why she persists, the woman I thought

I would be. Motherhood isn't a John Lewis advert, any more than reindeer can fly. I know this, but still, on my bad days I feel like a Father Christmas in a carpark on some windswept industrial estate, white beard slipping down to reveal a ginger moustache. The donkey won't wear its antlers, rain has fused the fairy lights, and it's only a matter of time until the authorities appear to shut the whole sorry enterprise down.

But still, my children believe.

Recently, I've been forcing myself to invite other women backstage, and now my phone pings all day and throughout the night, missives winging between worlds – *I told her not to hit him and so she thumped him with her Barbie; someone is hiding poos in the oven; it's oozing green stuff but he won't let me touch it; what do I do now?*

Maybe we should just admit that we don't know. All the mothers, rising up as one. We're sorry and we've tried. Kick away the pedestal, tear the cardigan in two.

I imagine those small upturned faces, their expressions. And I know that I can't. Not yet. Maybe not ever.

Until the day I do.

It's everything and nothing, the way it always is – tea is running late because Rainbows ended early and Netflix has crashed and it's not his, it's hers and why did he break it and she should give it back and hot teething cheeks and crusts of snot and swollen nappies and yesterday's porridge and it's a mess, my creation, just wretched, the whole experiment a failure. The clouds roll in and this is too much, too hard, I don't know what to do, what to say, and even if I did, no one would listen.

They scamper from me as I storm and howl, sweeping toys and plates and board books and the rest before me. Why did I ever think I could do this? This is the end. I am done.

Light footsteps, slamming doors, and I stand in heaving silence, picturing dark water rising, higher, ever higher, swallowing it all.

I could run away, throw my phone in the bin and get on a train, a plane, put half a planet between us. I could walk out the front door and just keep going.

I might even have opened it, inhaled the cold air.

But I can't go back. My children don't understand who I once was, because she is gone, left as the first child arrived. Wherever she is now, you can't get there from Heathrow.

Oh, I miss that woman, her energy, her ambition and, most of all, her certainty. And in the aching silence, I think of all the things I do not know. I think of them as I turn back to the sitting room, and then, a little later, as I tap quietly on the bedroom door and my daughter springs into my arms.

'I knew you'd come,' she says.

I don't know what colour it is at the end of the universe or how the cartoons get into the TV. I don't know why the pasta that was fine yesterday is inedible today.

'How did you know?' I ask her.

She looks up at me and smiles. 'I just did.'

Summer

'Marianne. Marianne!'

My husband's voice is shaking with . . . could it possibly be . . . delight?

It is seven-fifteen in the morning. With two small and hungry children, delight is, at this hour, unusual.

'Come and look, quick,' he says, and in his arms, the two-year-old echoes, 'Come! Come!'

They are peering into the plastic tank that sits on the bookcase, a tank which I am ashamed to say could do with a clean.

'What?'

'Fishy and Buddi have had a baby!'

And oh my God, they have. These two fish have, after a year together, produced a single tiny miniature, a dot of life, and for a few minutes, all regular morning activity, the toothbrushing and toileting and the doing of hair, it is all put on hold as we stare into the tank, and we are molten with joy.

After the death of our cat, I wanted to do something. Night after night, our daughter would weep. 'I just miss him,' she said, although, in the middle of that first lock-down, I had no way of knowing how much of the missing was for the cat and how much for her school, her friends, her whole pre-pandemic life.

The thought of another cat was just too much, and be-sides, it felt vaguely disrespectful to replace the grumpy, foul-mannered old tomcat with a delightful ball of fluff.

'When our loved ones die, we don't automatically get new ones,' I told my family. So instead, we queued out-side Pets at Home and came away with a plastic bag and two fish. Not goldfish, the tank I'd bought was deemed too small. Instead, the pet shop allowed us a pair of platys, which are like goldfish but simpler and more compact, without as much expression – basically, less good.

The black and gold one was assigned to our son, and was named Buddi after his favourite TV show. My daugh-ter claimed the pretty orange fish, naming her Delphie.

'I love her,' she said, nose pressed to the plastic, watch-ing, day by day, week by week, as Delphie frolicked with her little friend, slowed, sickened, and then, one night, made her inevitable way to the great fish tank in the sky.

'We'll get another one,' I said, when my daughter no-ticed that Delphie was gone. 'Tomorrow, we'll go straight over and buy a replacement.'

'Didn't you say that when our loved ones die we don't automatically—' my husband began, but I kept talking.

'Maybe not even one, but two.'

'Two?' said my husband.

'Fish insurance.'

★

The second trip was not nearly so ecstatic as the first, but we came home with two more platys, one almost transparent, his entire digestive tract on show, and one that familiar carroty orange.

'What shall we call the see-through one?' I said to my son.

He did not turn from the television.

'The FISH,' I said. 'WHAT DO YOU WANT TO CALL YOUR NEW FISH?'

'Fishy.'

'OK.'

My daughter put her hand on my arm. 'I am having the orange one, aren't I?'

'Of course,' I said. 'We could even call her Delphie?'

My daughter looked – rightly – appalled.

'Fair enough,' I said. 'How about Delphie Two?'

The two new fish were tipped into the tank to join the bereaved Buddi, and we waited, and watched. At first, it was lovely, three tiny bodies rippling through the water, in and out of the plants. The tank was full of life once more; fish surfacing and diving, threading between the reeds, shoaling and splitting and regrouping, pecking the gravel, pecking each other, repeatedly, two of them ganging up on the fish that was bright orange, who swam less and less and then went to cower behind a plant.

'Is she . . . happy?' said my daughter.

'Oh yes,' I said. 'Nibbling each other is just a thing that fish do. Go and get ready for bed.'

'She just doesn't seem like she's happy.'

No. She seemed like a fish who was being bitten to death.

'I'll sort it,' I said.

A few hours later, and the as-yet-unnamed-but-definitely-not-Delphie-Two was barely managing to stay afloat. 'Fuck's sake,' I muttered, filling a water jug. 'It is completely absurd that the happiness of the entire household rests on one tiny fish.'

My husband did not say, 'This was your idea,' for which I remain grateful.

Once the orange fish was moved into a jug, things settled. The pair in the tank simmered down. A second tank was set up for the orange outcast and installed in my daughter's bedroom. 'I'll name her Freyda,' said my daughter.

'How pretty,' I said. 'Why Freyda?'

'Because she is so afraid.'

'Great!'

'Do you think she's lonely?' I asked my husband, watching Freyda mooch in her tank. 'Maybe I should try and get her a friend, too?' Before he could say anything, my mind had run on. 'Then again, if the new fish bullies her, too, we'd have to get another tank and then we'd have three fish tanks and that would be too much, I suppose. Sorry, Freyda.'

Both Freyda and my husband remained silent.

The upside to fish is that, even accounting for all of the above, they are fairly undemanding pets.

The downside is that they don't do any of the things one wants, pet-wise. Not furry, with no discernible personality (and if anyone can intuit personality in something, it is me) and they can't even be held. The best thing platys do is create extraordinarily long trails of poo.

So the fish became another chore. 'Fed the fish?' we'd text each other. Occasionally, while watching TV of an evening, an indignant splosh would remind us that our tank had pretty much become a small and increasingly murky square of wallpaper.

Until today.

The baby fish is tiny, maybe five millimetres long, surprisingly vigorous for something that's all eyes and tail. 'We'll call her Summer,' says my daughter. 'She's so cute.'

Posting Summer's picture on social media, because if anything is designed for Instagram, surely it's this, I wait for the likes to roll in. Instead, three minutes later, someone says, 'Don't they eat their young?'

I google it. They do.

'Once the mother gives birth', says wikiHow, 'you can expect to have 20–40 new fry on average. Sometimes, this number can climb as high as 80.'

We look with fresh eyes at Buddi and Fishy, and I wonder what terrible atrocity took place in the night. I might be a bad mother, but at least I'm not as bad as that. Poor Summer now seems less like a beloved new member of our happy fishy family and more like the sole survivor of a massacre.

'Consider a separate tank,' says wikiHow and I race to the kitchen cupboard for an ice-cream tub.

'Is she still there?' I'm rummaging frantically, rummaging as I've never rummaged in my life, for Summer's life. 'Is she OK?'

'Yes,' yells my daughter. 'Not eaten. Yet.'

Summer is placed in a vessel all of her own and enjoys a solitary meal of powdered fish food.

Fishy and Buddi carry on with their lives. They do not seem aware that they've just lost their baby. They don't seem especially aware of anything.

Upstairs, Freyda glowers in the corner of her tank. Maybe, when Summer is bigger, they can move in together.

'And then maybe Summer and Freyda will have babies!' cries my daughter, ecstatically, and I can see how, within mere months, the whole thing will turn into a cross between a Spanish soap opera and a Greek tragedy, so I cut short any further conversation and pack her off to school.

Buddi and Delphie (RIP) and Fishy and Fredya and now, tiny Summer.

Making a cup of coffee, I pause to peer in at her.

'You've got to stay alive,' I say, sternly. 'You may not know it, but you are important.'

Summer comes to the surface to nibble a leftover flake. She might be smaller than the nail on my little finger, but she swims with confidence, panache, even. She does not need to be told that she is important. She knows.

So I return to work, thinking how strange it is that the happiness of an entire household can rest upon this speck of life, upon the shoulders of something that doesn't even have shoulders. How strange, how absurd. How completely wonderful.

The Shape of Things to Come

'This,' I would say, 'is a blue triangle. Blue triangle.' My little boy would place it, thoughtfully, into his mouth. Then, 'Square. Green square.' And I would take his hand and feed the chunk of plastic through the correct shape in the lid of his box of coloured blocks. *Clunk.* 'See? It fits.'

Copying, he would try the square against the triangular slot, jabbing it over and over. 'It goes in this one,' I would say, guiding him up. 'Square. Four corners. One, two, three, four.'

He would reach for the triangle.

'And this has three points. Look. One, two, three.'

The box was good for a narrow window of time, a couple of months at best, before my son became entirely adept at slotting in the pieces, *clunk clunk clunk.* Finished. Done.

So, one day, I brought home a cheap kaleidoscope I'd found in the charity shop at the top of the road. It was with slight trepidation that I presented it to the kids, aware that I was perilously close to being *that* person, the one telling them that a skipping rope is much more fun than an iPad, I mean, honestly, you lot don't know how good you've got it these days, etc.

But, surprisingly, it was a hit, so much that they even fought over it. 'Magic patterns,' my daughter said, squinting hard into the hole. 'I made a good one! Quick, look,' and then as the slightest tilt changed her view once more, 'Oh. Make it come back?'

'It's just the mirrors reflecting triangles and rectangles and squares,' I told her. 'If we keep shaking it, we'll get more patterns.'

'The same ones?'

'They'll never be quite the same. But that's what makes it so lovely.'

Even as she was processing this, the toddler had grabbed the cardboard tube and was holding it triumphantly aloft.

'I was playing with it,' screamed my daughter, but he was shouting back, 'Shake!' and it was all so loud and so fast and I should have seen it coming but I didn't; I never do.

'Shake! Shake! Shake!'

When I was twenty-four, I encountered the first of the children I never had: unborn, unconceived, but still, somehow, there. And ever since, I have thought about the children that never quite were.

The winter I almost saw my almost-child, my flatshare was spacious, but so damp that my clothes grew white fur; the area was close to the Tube but a hotspot for prostitutes. Coming back late from the night bus, I would step between the pimps that stood guard by the block where I lived; in the mornings, the doorstep would be strewn with condoms that pooled like jellyfish, milky and spent.

And it was around about then that I was lucky enough to find myself in a room with a nurse who knew about contraception, really knew about it, and how to talk about it, in that she was aware of both what I needed to know and what I wanted to know. Best of all, she had twenty minutes free just for me.

There's not much I remember about her, not her face, or her clothes, but I do recall that she was kind, and interested. Most of all (and I hesitate a little to use the word but can find none better) she was motherly, in that she combined knowledge with a gentle authority. Simply sitting opposite her was reassuring, and reassurance was something I craved.

I am struggling to remember what had taken me into that particular clinic, or quite what was going on in my life at the time. I must have been seeing someone, needed something. There'd been a man, there was usually a man, which meant there was sex, but never any discussion of what that might mean should things not go as planned.

I look back on my young adulthood, the weighing scales and the blood pressure cuffs, this pill and then that, and think how I moulded myself to be what I thought I should be. How I ensured that I was fertile in appearance but not in actual fact. It was my job to worry about getting pregnant and to prevent it. The men, as far as I could tell, simply assumed it wouldn't happen.

So the feeling I had, talking to this nurse, was, most of all, that of relief. There was a woman in the driving seat, and while it wasn't ideal that it was someone I had never met before and might not again, at least there *was* someone, because it certainly wasn't me. Together, we went through everything, injections and implants, each coil and pill.

'And then there's the cap,' I remember her saying. 'But I don't usually recommend that unless it's for a married woman who doesn't mind whether she gets pregnant or not.'

It was one of the most astonishing things I had ever heard. Who *doesn't mind* getting pregnant? It was a statement I might have dismissed as insanity, had it not come from a woman who had earned my absolute trust; a woman who, I had decided five minutes before, knew better than me.

I carried her words for years. If they had been written on a piece of paper it would have been folded in many places, creases coming apart and corners furred. There are women out there who don't mind whether they get pregnant or not. Women crowded by great clusters of invisible almost children, children who at any moment might slip into being.

Then again, wasn't I the same, really? Aren't so many of us with ovaries and a womb the same, the condom positioned maybe three minutes later than it should have been, the tiny tablets that, if not quite missed, are taken half a day later than is specified by the instructions on the pack. That's before we even get to the abortions and the miscarriages, to the morning-after pill pinching out sparks before they flutter into flames.

The man and I might just have had sex; my memory is not entirely clear. But I can picture the room, the particular cool blue of the walls, the bubble of light from the bedside table.

We were discussing names. He liked names from literature. I said that I preferred nature, names of trees and flowers. There was a beat, and there it was, the next stage of the discussion, waiting. It seemed to me that a child was waiting, too, in the wings of the night, listening hard for the words that might call it into being.

Instead, the moment passed. And the child retreated back into the dark.

For the first eighteen months of my daughter's life, we were a new family; she, my husband and me: it was plenty, a surfeit, even. Everything was hard, hard beyond describing, but it was full. If there was a slot, it was the shape of us, and through we went.

And. Only. Also.

There was never enough money, or patience, or sleep, or time. Days began with a lurch of terror and never seemed to be over. My husband's work was rocky, mine, as ever, precarious, and ours was the kind of baby who only ever wanted to be held. ('You've made a rod for your own back with that one,' said the sibyls of M&S.) I felt an increasing awareness that, if there was a trajectory that everyone else seemed to be on, a sort of conveyor belt into happily ever after, I did not seem to be on it with them.

Anyway, it wasn't just work, or our daughter's age, or money. Or rather, it was all those things, and it was everything else. While everyone around me shrugged and got on with it, I seemed snared in the terror of looking after a newborn, for all that my daughter had turned two, could even imagine herself, one day, at three. Everything was too hard, and it wasn't her, and it wasn't my husband. It was me.

Still. 'You're not pregnant, are you?' said a friend, as we watched our toddlers playing in a paddling pool.

'Does he make you feel broody?' asked a new mother, as I held her baby.

'You must have another one,' said the man who worked in the post office. The post office! Where we (he) discussed my reproductive future with all the ease and authority of the in-law at the wedding who's just drained their third glass of warm white wine. 'You must not wait. It's better for her, better for you.'

If I conceived a baby tomorrow, I calculated, in the small hours of the night, or standing at the sink, or wrestling my screaming child into the buggy, then the gap between them would be three years. The same as me and my sister, which, while it wasn't the two years, or even eighteen months of some that I knew, was a childhood shared. It would be respectable enough. Then we'd be finished. Out of this no man's land and into the blessed future.

Of course, that was assuming I could conceive quickly and stay pregnant, none of which was a given. Opening up to the possibility of another pregnancy meant the potential for a miscarriage, or stillbirth, which I knew I could not even begin to bear. And the discussion, once more, about whether we could parent a child with grave health issues, were that to be the case. And then, if everything went as well as it possibly could, and with my fortieth birthday approaching, it was more of an 'if' than the first time around, but if everything went exactly as we were hoping it might, we'd have a beautiful, perfect new child. And I knew I couldn't bear that, either.

Month by month, moment to moment, my conscious brain ran endless, barmy equations whose integers' values shifted like the currency markets; graphs that could change within a fraction of a second, rendering any final value obsolete even before it came.

'We can operate,' said the consultant I'd visited to fix the damage wrought by my daughter's birth. 'But we always wait until the woman has completed her family. Otherwise there is every chance we'll need to do it again.' He looked down at my notes. 'Do you plan to have any more children?'

We took trips to the zoo. To Kew Gardens. We went on holiday and when my daughter found a friend to play with on the beach, I hid behind my book, for watching them together was agony.

Our dining table was designed for four, and oh, how I came to loathe the sight of that empty, recriminating chair. I found myself seeking out places where the seats came in odd numbers; those trains with three seats facing two. Circular tables. The back of the car.

'Are we nearly there yet, Mummy? Are we nearly there?'

'The reason to have more than one child,' an ex once told me, grandly (he was, generally, quite grand), 'is so that there are people to share your care when you get old.'

I remembered this, contemplated an image of my tiny girl as a grown woman, on the phone to the old people's

home, concerned about my pressure sores or that no one
had shaved her dad in days. I thought about Lynn Barber,
who wrote about her daughter coming to the hospital
when her husband was dying, the smart click of her kitten
heels.

And I thought, we are too old for her *now*.

Conversations were either with her or with one another, leaving her sitting and waiting for us to finish. Our
two adult lives bore down upon her, the weight of our
cares balanced upon a single point. 'Play with me?' she
would say, and I would try, for all that my attempts at
childlike silliness felt flat, transactions in a currency that
was not my own.

'This is all in your head,' my husband pointed out,
ever reasonable, as we observed our happy, smiley, chatty
daughter. 'She's perfectly OK.'

How strange, then, that what I wanted was for her to
tumble and pinch and shriek. For life to roar back at her,
at us, to buffet and toss my little family, to challenge my
carefully wrought status quo. Broken dolls, screaming
rows, pulled hair, that was what childhood ought to be, I
thought, and instead, we had a two-year-old who thought
nothing of falling into step with the adults, who seemed
to think she was one herself.

On the days we went to see her grandparents, the
imbalance seemed more apparent still. We four adults
vied for her attention as though her youth was a precious
spring from which to drink. The love, the fascination
with every word she uttered . . . collectively, we were
almost vampiric.

I would excuse myself, go and lie down, and in my

eyeline would be the wardrobe where, not having a loft, we'd stashed every discarded toy, every outgrown piece of clothing, 'just in case'. We could have kept it all in our house, but really, I could not bear the wordless reproach of each rattle and folded muslin; I had to get them out and away. 'It's getting very full,' my father-in-law said gently, watching us trying to ram yet another Bag for Life onto an upper shelf.

Meanwhile, there was plenty to read, and almost none of it was helpful. 'You will be amazed at your capacity to expand your energy', said the articles, which seemed to imply I had some energy to begin with. 'You will be surprised at just how much you can love.' These tended to be written by the same people whose other articles said things like, 'Birth is hard but the moment they place your newborn in your arms you'll realise that it was all worth it!'

They like exclamation marks, these writers. My journalist husband tells me that in his trade they are known as 'screamers'. They nuzzle up alongside phrases like, 'You've got to laugh, haven't you?' and, 'You must treasure these moments. Blink and your baby will be gone.'

'Must.' 'Got to.' I had to be the woman who is content with a single child, or the woman who sallies forth towards a second pregnancy with a sanguine smile; for no one I know has ever said, 'I was desperate for another, but I couldn't bring myself to do it.' Or, 'I have two children, and my life is harder now, the space for my adult self is smaller, and I don't know if it was worth it,' or, 'I made a decision, and it was wrong.'

Once taken, the choices seem to calcify into a kind of inevitability, at least as seen from the outside. Perhaps it's because, a few years on, the outcome feels inevitable? If a child has been conceived, the only socially admissible stance is that the blessing of it is so great as to eclipse all else, even, especially, the mother. It has to be worth it – anything else is unsayable, unthinkable, even.

Still, the outcome did not seem inevitable to me, the months ticking past, the gap between my actual child and the notional one yawning larger and then larger still.

Having a child is a woman's choice. It is about you, it is all about you, and then, very quickly, it is not about you at all. Which is why it felt profoundly selfish to think about myself, so much so that I could only really bring myself to express the decision in terms of how it might affect the child I already had.

I would be a less good mother, that much seemed clear; less time, less energy, less patience. ('You will discover that your patience is bottomless, along with your love', cooed the articles. No, no.) But the trade-off is a new brother or sister. A sibling for my girl, an eternal playmate. Someone who will be there when I can do no more. Not that the world is exactly short of people, but to have someone else, one other person on the planet who is made of the same stuff, someone who understands what it is to live under this roof with us, right here and now.

The logic is nuts, and obviously so. You are having a baby to 'give' your first child a sibling. The new one is being treated as though it's a kind of supplicant offering, not an equal and a whole other person, which it is. Or rather, would be, because this child does not yet exist, and might not, ever.

And then, the thoughts that came in the night. To have another child would be to step back into the hall of mirrors once more, to bend and stretch, to surrender to hormones and milk and blood, and that place holds no attraction, not for me. Yes, five, ten, twenty years down the line, I would be grateful for having undergone the experience. That still left the bit in-between.

'I always knew I wanted lots,' said someone I know. Said various people I know, in fact. Or, 'I always knew I wanted one.' What, I wondered, had I always known?

If pushed, really pushed, I'll admit that there is, in my mind, a hall, or a cloakroom, and in it a great tangle of hats and coats and bags. It's a mess that, in reality, would drive me mad, so I don't know why it's so alluring. In this half-formed fantasy I think maybe I'm next door, doling out burnt soup to the hungry masses, all windblown curls and pink cheeks. Or maybe I *am* the cloakroom, encompassing the mess, loving it, every crumb of dirt and each individual finger of every muddy glove.

One child seemed just within the boundary of my control. More than one would tip me straight over the edge, and into . . . where? Acceptance? Insanity? Could I settle in this land, pick a point somewhere between love and madness to build a home, of floury fingerprints and potato paintings and hands thrown up in a kind of ecstatic despair? Ah, to be set free, with more of everything, more mayhem, more heartbeats, more opinions that were not my own; for my opinions, at that point, did not seem up to much, even to me.

'When you've got two then just looking after one feels like a holiday' was a phrase I heard more than once. 'They were going for one more to finish up,' I was told, 'and then they had twins. Now they have three kids under two and they're just broken.' My grandpa was a twin. They run in families.

The mother I wanted to be, fun and fizzy, shambolic, overwhelmed with love, she did not have one child. The mother I *was* – a rigid, frigid perfectionist – she sat on her nice sofa, acting the part so well, with only the occasional leak of tears to signify that she was not coping, patently not, with a single gorgeous toddler. She had not quite lost her grip on her former life and self, clinging on, lashed by motherhood's waves. Perhaps a second child would loosen her grasp.

So jump, I thought, as my fingers gripped tighter still.

'You don't have to have another,' they said, the few I could bear to take into my confidence. Then, when my reaction made it clear that this wasn't the right thing to say, they asked, 'What do you want? What do you want right now?'

The answer was that I wanted . . . not to be myself. I wanted to be someone – anyone – else. Someone who had more children, yes, or a woman happy and messy and open and content amidst the wonderful family she was lucky enough to have already.

I'm glad that I didn't dismiss those women who didn't mind whether they got pregnant or not, even if I couldn't understand them. Two years after the birth of my daughter, that woman was me. For I'd got it wrong, or at least, not quite right; it wasn't that I didn't mind whether I had another child, it was simply that I could not make the decision. I wanted the decision made for me. Or, I made the decision, over and over, a million times a day, and it was both at once. For two things can both be true even if it appears not. A woman can/can't want to get pregnant. She should/shouldn't. Schrödinger's baby.

Now, and only now, it occurs to me that maybe if a choice seems impossible, it's not because of the chooser. Maybe it's that the pressures upon her are too great. I berate myself for not being the mother I wanted to be and, yes, maybe a fair proportion of the fault is my own, if 'fault' is even the right word. But while it is me, it's not just me. It's living in the world, and the world is hard. It's hard for everyone.

I watched, and I waited. I became the woman I do not much like, observing the hand that strayed to the belly, the extra caress from a partner, the friend who let the wine sit untouched in her glass. I noted who was stashing their buggy, and who was giving it away. Who announced they were going to move out of the city for more space, or 'do' the loft.

And everyone was pregnant.

Or at least, that was how it seemed. Go to any nursery at pick-up time and they're everywhere, small neat bumps and great big bellies and tiny new babies *waaah-waaah-waaahing* in the hallway. The friends we had made because all our first babies were due at the same time rose and fell with their second children, each according to some internal rhythm that seemed almost tidal in its timing and inevitability.

What a mad thing it is, to have a second child. To have any child, come to that, but a second child most of all, knowing what you do.

'The thing is,' said one friend, 'it's really not a big deal.'

I had to stop myself from yelling. It IS a big deal. It's a whole other human being. There is no deal bigger.

'I have a sister,' said my daughter.

It turned out that she was talking about the little girl who lived next door.

'She's not your sister,' I said, eventually, after people at nursery started asking about this other child. 'You don't have a sister.'

'Yes, I do,' said my daughter.

And even though I shook my head, I knew she would be a girl, the next baby, my daughter remixed, curly and sweet and silly and serious and small.

Female foetuses, I learned, have all their eggs in place by twenty weeks, the next generation readying itself before the woman who might usher it forth has even taken a breath. Unlike men, who produce sperm day by day, in endless renewal, I have carried the beginnings of these children quite literally through every sexual encounter. My children, my grandchildren, even. All those brothers and sisters.

When I think of eggs, I think of children, of small hands rooting through straw, of wooden spoons and cake batter. Eggs as children, though?

A friend has frozen her eggs. When we talked about it, she laughed and put on a high voice: 'We're cold, Mummy!'

Another friend has a photo of her baby from back when she was just six cells. Her little girl has a maybe sibling, waiting in a laboratory freezer. The veil that separates these children from our world is meltingly thin.

'A sister,' said my daughter, kissing the forehead of her baby doll.

Sometimes, in the park, or at other people's houses, I thought I heard her. Believed that if I could just turn my head fast enough I might see her racing past, legs whirring to catch up with her big sister, and I wanted to grab her, take her shoulders in my hands, brush her fringe from her face and look deep into her green–blue eyes.

Each month, a half child, my half of a child, gone.

What we think about, when we think about having children, is so private and undiscussed that even ordering my own thoughts seems invasive and strange. One either is or isn't a parent. There either isn't, or is, a child. The in-between is not something we can grasp.

Children never question themselves in this way. They simply are, like oxygen and gravity. It's only us adults who think in these terms, those with the power to call them forth. Now that I have had children, know the specific texture of the children that my husband and I produce, the squash of the nose and the kink of the hair, I mourn the children I will not have. I might have met these children in the hinterlands of consciousness, seen their faces flit between the photos in family albums, the tip of a chin, the curve of a nostril. Sometimes I believe that I may meet them still.

All those children, my children, that I won't get to watch unfurl. I see my friends with two boys or two girls, and it makes me want to shake the kaleidoscope once again, shake it over and over, tear down whatever separates me from the warm and clinging bodies of the babies that could be mine.

Soon my own children will grow large and their small selves will be gone, too; their tiny hands and crusted noses, their beloved idioms, their hot tears and quick smiles living on only in memory. I look back through my phone at their faces from just a couple of years ago, imagine them somehow taking flight and joining together with all the babies I will never have. That's what they're seeing, isn't it, the women who stop short in the café to gaze into strangers' buggies? The babies, all the babies.

Can I kick them out, my gaggle of little ghosts? Do I even want to?

A year after I had my boy, I had a coil put in. A coil with a ten-year lifespan, that will take me beyond fifty. The clinic was in Soho. Everyone was cool, smart, smiley and good-looking, and afterwards, because we still had a child-free hour and Chinatown was just over the road, my husband and I even went out for a celebratory lunch.

No more breastfeeding, we said, over green beans and crispy duck. Teething? Finished! We have all that we need. We are complete. Bin the cloudy bottles, give the steriliser away. A family of four, a tidy square, balanced and even. No more babies, ever.

I sit, now, in the sunshine, writing this. The walls are white, the desk is clear. My son is at nursery and my daughter, at school. After the lockdowns, after the years of babyhood, after everything, I've had to fight so hard, for this room, this chair, the time to sit and type. I don't want another line on the pregnancy test, another kid banging on the door, another eighteen months out of my life and then the forced re-entry, the dicing of myself into slice upon painful slice, sharing out all of me, never enough. I don't want another child. I don't.

But, just for a moment, bring them in, all the children I will never have. Let them crowd this small room. Let them spin in the chair, knock over my water, let them scream and gossip, fight and console. Let them fill me up, fill the world, these gorgeous, beautiful children.

All those children, waiting. I don't want them, I don't. And oh, but I do.

Acknowledgements

With thanks to:

Shelley Harris, Jo Harkin, Alison Davidson, Beth Morrey, Deirdre Mask, Emma Beddington, Gavanndra Hodge, Katherine Rundell, Piers Torday, Matthew Holness, Anna Gorringe, Mary-Ann Ochota, Alex Reeve, Deborah Lee, Susie Mesure, Anna Mazzola, Emma Flint, Adi Bloom, Neil Blackmore, Alix Christie, Yojana Sharma, Tammy Cohen, Cathy De'Freitas, Lucy Nicholson, Alice Jones, Rebecca Armstrong, Sarah Carson, Rob Hastings, Rupert Hawksley, Madévi Dailly, Perdita Cargill, Caroline Jones, Tor Udall, Alice Broadway, all at JULA, Chrissy Ryan and Rosie Pierce.

At Orion, thank you to Kate Moreton, Francesca Pearce, Katie Moss, Sarah Fortune, Steve Marking, Emma Ewbank, Hannah Cox and Paul Stark.

To my agent Felicity Blunt and my editor Francesca Main, thank you, thank you.

And thank you to R, W and O.

This book was written with the support of a Work In Progress grant from The Society of Authors and the Authors' Foundation, for which I am hugely grateful.

Sources of Quotations

The Mothers

'there were women and there were mothers . . .', Anne Enright, *Making Babies* (London: Jonathan Cape, 2004), 13

Mr Skinny Legs

'You just have to Google childbirth . . .', 'Pregnancy phobia is being "driven by social media"', BBC 5 Live, 13 September 2018

'I've been through childbirth three times . . .', 'How much does it hurt?', Mosaic, 10 January 2017

'One brilliant consultant tells her trainees . . .', Adam Kay, *This is Going to Hurt* (London: Picador, 2017), 239

'Women with a high to severe fear of childbirth . . .', M.A. O'Connell, A.S. Khashan, P. Leahy-Warren, F. Stewart,

S.M. O'Neill, 'Interventions for fear of childbirth including tocophobia', *Cochrane Database of Systematic Reviews* 2021; 7

Flesh and Blood

'Kuhirwa, a young female mountain gorilla. . .', 'Winning images announced for Wildlife Photographer of the Year 2018', Natural History Museum, 17 October 2018

High Wire

'Using a net has a tendency. . .', 'Fairly Curious: Why Don't the Flying Wallendas Use a Safety Net?', Curious Louisville, 22 August 2017

'Oh! I am terrified . . .', Phillipe Petit, *To Reach the Clouds* (London: Faber & Faber, 2015), 19

Some Discomfort

'Women receive little information in advance about episiotomy. . .', He S, Jiang H, Qian X, et al, 'Women's experience of episiotomy: a qualitative study from China', *BMJ Open* 2020; 10